SAILMATE

HOW TO
PAINT YOUR
BOAT

PAINTING • VARNISHING • ANTIFOULING

Second edition

NIGEL CLEGG

SHERIDAN HOUSE

This edition published 2006
by Sheridan House Inc.
145 Palisade Street
Dobbs Ferry, NY 10522
www.sheridanhouse.com

First edition published 1997 by Sheridan House, Inc.

Note: While all reasonable care has been taken in the publication
of this book, the publisher takes no responsibility for the use of the
methods or products described in the book.

A CIP catalogue record for this book is available
from the Library of Congress, Washington, DC.

ISBN 1-574509-223-5

Printed and bound in Great Britain

Introduction

The phrase 'like watching paint dry' is often used to describe the most boring or unremarkable events in life; but while painting may be very much an everyday occurrence, some of the processes involved are remarkably complex – indeed, many are not yet fully understood.

It would be true to say that paint is only noticed when it looks outstandingly good or outstandingly bad, but at most other times it is simply taken for granted. With a little thought, though, we soon realise that paint coatings are an integral part of our modern-day life, whether they are used to coat food or drink cans, the cars that we drive, or the goods that we buy in the shops.

However, the demands made of yacht coatings are unusually severe, with the harsh marine environment posing challenges that no household or automotive paint would ever face. Moreover, yacht paints have to withstand the wear and tear of being walked on, having ropes and chains dragged across them, not to mention fender wear and occasional pilot error! These demands have led to the development of many high performance paints which, although rather 'technical' in their application, can protect and beautify for many years.

By understanding the principles involved, painting can be a satisfying and rewarding experience. This understanding should also help to avoid expensive and time-consuming mistakes, which do little to endear us to repair and maintenance chores. This is particularly important to professionals, to whom time is money, and mistakes are expensive.

The aim of this book is to take some of the mystery out of painting, and to explain in a straightforward manner why certain practices are adopted, and why (for instance) correct film thickness, overcoating intervals, and good application conditions are so important. By explaining what is actually happening, readers can see for themselves what they are trying to achieve, and how, perhaps, they could do it better.

The all-important subject of health and safety is also addressed, with common-sense advice on how to work safely, with explanations of relevant health and safety terminology.

Finally, the book contains a useful 'Glossary of Painting Terms'; this explains many of the painting and technical terms used. There is also a 'Fault Finding' section, for when things go wrong.

Having answered many thousands of technical queries on the telephone and by letter, I have endeavoured to cover all of the most common yacht painting questions, while providing sufficient background information for readers to solve some of the more obscure problems themselves.

In short, the book is like a personal telephone helpline, available 24 hours a day, and never engaged!

Nigel Clegg

Acknowledgements

Grateful thanks are owed to those companies who helped in the production of this book by providing information and photographs, or by allowing photographs to be taken. Listed in alphabetical order, these are:

    Blakes Marine Paints
    DeVilbiss Ransburg Industrial Painting Equipment
    Hodge Clemco, Surface Preparation Equipment
    International Yacht Paints
    Marineware (Distributors of Awlgrip and Epifanes paints
    in the UK)
    MG Duff, Cathodic Protection Engineers
    Resinous Chemicals Ltd
    The Marine Biological Association, Plymouth, England
    Devonport Royal Dockyard Limited

Finally, special thanks are due to my wife Lynda for her encouragement and great patience during the long days and nights of writing, and our young children Jonathan and Rebecca, without whose 5 am alarm calls I would never have finished!

Back to basics | 1

Before we start looking at paints in any detail, we should remind ourselves of some basic rules for safe and successful painting:

- A paint scheme is only as good as its weakest coat: painting on top of badly prepared surfaces, or over an old scheme that is unsound, is a waste of both time and money.
- Many marine substrates are better not painted at all than painted badly.
- Always use the right material for the job: trying to cut corners by using cheaper alternatives will often result in failure, and will cost far more in the long term.
- Don't try to save money by thinning the paint unnecessarily: if the manufacturers thought they could save money in that way, they would have done it themselves!
- *Always* apply the number of coats specified by the manufacturer: reducing the number of coats will reduce both the performance and the lifespan of the coating scheme.
- *All* organic coatings (including epoxies and polyurethanes) are slightly moisture permeable. This means that paint cannot be used to 'seal up' rot, corrosion, or a blistering glassfibre hull.
- Only use products specified for underwater use on yacht bottoms: some yacht paints will fail if applied to permanently wet areas, so check first.
- *Always* read and follow the manufacturer's instructions: they are there for a reason.
- Paints are chemical compositions, and must be handled with care and respect: think about health and safety before you start work.
- If in doubt, *ask!*

The rationale for some of these points may not be immediately obvious, but as you read through this book, their importance should become increasingly clear.

This would also be a good opportunity to introduce some of the more important terms that we shall be using: the word **coating** is now widely used to describe both paints and varnishes, especially where differences between the two types of material are not significant. The word **paint** is generally accepted to mean a pigmented or coloured coating, while a **varnish** is usually an unpigmented, clear coating.

The term **conventional coating** usually describes a single-component paint or varnish that dries by absorbing oxygen from the atmosphere, but can also include coatings that dry by solvent evaporation – such as antifoulings, and some keel primers.

High performance coatings are usually chemically cured, two-component products like epoxies and polyurethanes, which provide much improved mechanical, chemical and cosmetic properties.

Once applied, each coat of paint or varnish is called a *film*, and a series of films is called a **coating scheme**. The thickness of both paint films and schemes is measured either in microns (abbreviated μ or μM), or, less commonly now, in thousandths of an inch (usually called *Mil* or *Thou*)[1]. Unless stated otherwise, this measurement refers to the thickness of coatings when they are fully dried and cured (ie their *dry film thickness* or *DFT*), rather than their *wet film thickness*.

A Glossary of Painting Terms starts on page 128, while Conversion Tables for metric, US and imperial measures can be found on page 132.

---

[1] There are one million microns in a metre, and 2540 microns in an inch. One mil is equivalent to 25.4 microns or μM, while one micron is equivalent to 0.00003937 inch.

Personal Hygiene | 2
and Safety

Paints are chemical compositions, and must be handled with care and respect. In particular, the following precautions should always be observed when using paint products:

- Protect your eyes when mixing or using paints or solvents.
- Work in well ventilated conditions. Where this is not possible, the use of suitable respiratory protection is *essential*.
- *Never* work alone or in isolation when carrying out hazardous operations or working in hazardous areas; you may need help in the event of an emergency.
- Protect your hands whenever mixing or using paints or solvents by wearing suitable protective gloves. A barrier cream is recommended for added protection.
- Take care when opening paint tins, as the contents may be under pressure (especially polyurethane curing agents and paints containing aluminium). If a tin appears to be under pressure, cover it with a rag before opening to avoid the risk of splashing.
- *Never* touch your mouth, eyes or other sensitive areas when wearing gloves, or without washing your hands. Always wash your hands *before* visiting the toilet.
- *Never* use solvents for hand washing. Remove paint by washing with tepid water and a suitable hand cleaner from your chandler or an auto factor. A good hand cream should be applied after washing to maintain good skin condition.
- Wear protective overalls when handling, mixing or applying paint. Working clothes made from natural fibres are usually best as they dissipate sweat better than man-made materials. Elasticated cuffs and ankles are recommended when sanding to prevent the ingress of particles of irritating dust.
- *Never* put solvent-soaked or contaminated rags in the pockets of overalls, as these can cause serious skin disorders, and pose a severe fire hazard. Remove contaminated overalls immediately for the same reasons.

- Wear respiratory protection whenever sanding or scraping paint to avoid inhaling harmful dusts. The dust from epoxy fillers can be particularly irritating.
- *Antifoulings must never be dry sanded or burnt off* as they contain toxic compounds.
- *Never* eat or smoke when working with paint.
- Wash your hands, and rinse your mouth with fresh water before eating, drinking or smoking. Overalls should be removed before eating.
- Wash protective equipment regularly with soap and water to remove irritating materials and to discourage bacteria.

Please note that the information given here is only a brief résumé of the requirements for safe working conditions when painting, and is not intended to be exhaustive. If you have any concerns about health or safety, you should contact the paint manufacturer for further advice. If you are a professional painter, your local Health and Safety Executive will also be pleased to advise.

What is paint? | 3

Before looking at painting schemes or application details, we should first consider how paints are made; this will help our understanding of the properties and limitations of different coating types, and will also highlight some of the objectives and compromises involved in their formulation.

In its simplest form, a paint could be comprised of just a colouring pigment in water (like whitewash), although a coating like this would provide little protection in a marine environment, and would quickly be washed away by rain and sea water. However, if we add a resin to bind the particles of pigment together, our paint can be made far more weatherproof, and will provide much better protection for the substrate.

Unfortunately, most resins are either solid or very viscous at normal temperatures, so a solvent must be added to reduce viscosity before the paint can be manufactured or applied. There are other problems too: many resins would take days or even weeks to dry by themselves, so *dryers* have to be added to provide acceptable drying times. Similarly, many colouring pigments would have limited obliteration if used on their own, so *extenders* are added to improve opacity, and perhaps to give the paint a better feel or body.

While it is true that some excellent paint formulations have been dreamt up on a Friday afternoon, most are the result of years of painstaking work, usually involving hundreds of test panels and intensive exposure trials even before the first samples can be field tested. Fig 1 gives a basic idea of what a typical can of paint is likely to contain. So what are these constituents, and how are they used?

◆ RESINS

Known technically as the *vehicle* or *binder*, resins are the backbone of all paints and varnishes, and so usually lend their name to the paint as a generic type (ie alkyd, epoxy or polyurethane). As would be expected, resins have a profound effect on the properties of coatings, determining factors such as gloss and gloss retention, abrasion and chemical resistance, adhesion, moisture permeability and, to some extent, compatibility with other paint types.

The first function of a resin is to provide a vehicle for dispersed pigments and extenders, carrying them to the surface being painted; once

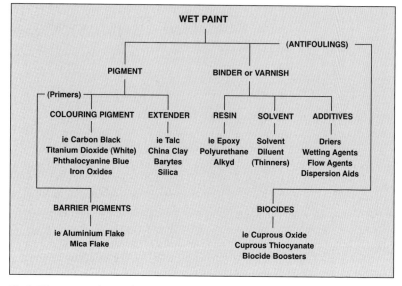

Fig 1 What a typical can of paint is likely to contain.

applied, the resin must change from a liquid into a solid, binding the pigments and extenders into a cohesive film, and bonding them to the substrate. To achieve this change, the resin undergoes a series of complex chemical reactions, where comparatively small, mobile molecules are joined together into long polymer chains by a process known as *curing*, *cross linking* or *polymerisation*.

Curing is principally a chemical reaction, so the degree of cure is very much dependent on temperature (and in some cases, relative humidity); therefore likely application conditions must always be borne in mind whenever a paint is being formulated or purchased.

While an in-depth discussion about film forming reactions is beyond the scope of this book, an understanding of the behaviour and limitations of different resin types is extremely helpful when choosing a paint or varnish for any particular project.

Conventional resins

The very first paints and varnishes were made from natural drying oils such as linseed (pressed from the seeds of the flax plant), and occasionally from fish oils. Resins made from natural drying oils are known as *oleoresins*.

Drying oils cure by absorbing large quantities of oxygen from the atmosphere to produce simple polymers, although this is a fairly slow process with many practical limitations. However, these oils are also very 'fatty' in nature, and are characterised by the high concentrations of linolenic, linoleic, oleic and other fatty acids that they contain. (Do you remember linoleum?) Chemists searching to overcome the limitations of drying oils found that these acids could be reacted with high molecular weight alcohols like pentaerythritol and glycerol to produce a type of (poly)*ester*, which had far better mechanical and chemical properties than their oleoresinous predecessors.

These new resins became known as *alkyds* (ie derived from an *acid* and an *alcohol*), and have provided the basis for the majority of varnishes and decorative paints from the early 1950s until the present day. They are still known as 'oil based' resins by many older painters, though this is not strictly correct.

The most immediate advantage of alkyd resins was their speed of drying and almost clear colour, but they also provided far superior gloss and durability. Alkyds can also be made from cheaper and more readily available vegetable oils such as sunflower, safflower and rape seed oils, although most good yacht coatings are still manufactured with soya, linseed and tung oils in the interests of quality and performance.

Like oleoresins, alkyds dry firstly by solvent evaporation, followed by reaction with atmospheric oxygen to form loosely linked polymers. This *oxidative* drying mechanism is ideal for yacht coatings, allowing prolonged storage in sealed containers and avoiding the need for separate curing agents.

This great simplicity has led to alkyds becoming very much the mainstay of yacht coatings, being easy to apply in most conditions, and combining good cosmetic appearance, protection and durability at reasonable cost.

For added convenience, drying can be accelerated by adding small quantities of metallic compounds (dryers) that increase the rate of oxidation. Traditionally, tiny quantities of lead compounds were used for this purpose, but recent health concerns have resulted in alternatives such as zinc, zirconium and cobalt being substituted. The presence of cobalt is often noticeable by the purple tint that it gives to some paints and varnishes, although this is not visible in the dried film.

Standard alkyd or conventional coatings provide more than adequate performance for most painting and varnishing jobs on board, and are also quite flexible for traditionally built boats where some movement can be

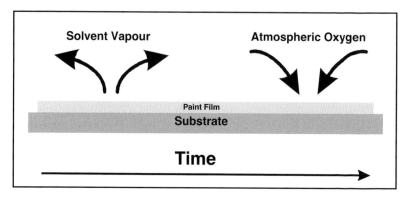

Fig 2 The conventional drying process.

expected. Their initial gloss is also very good at around 75–80 per cent, which is high enough to look superb on well prepared substrates, while avoiding the rather plastic appearance associated with two-pack polyurethanes.

Conventional finishes can be expected to retain their gloss and appearance for around two or three sailing seasons in temperate climates, or perhaps a single season in tropical or subtropical conditions, although precise predictions are always difficult. Ultraviolet light is one of the worst enemies of paint coatings and plastics, as it gradually destroys the chemical bonds in both resin and pigment, with the result that the coating surface breaks up into small fragments. Known technically as *ultraviolet degradation*, this effect is initially seen as dullness or a loss of gloss, but with time surfaces become chalky and completely drab. Climatic conditions inevitably have a major influence on the longevity of paint coatings, although industrial pollution and other local factors can also help to accelerate weathering effects.

White paints usually have the best gloss retention as their pigments reflect much of the ultraviolet energy to which they are exposed, although darker colours do not have this advantage. Moreover, darker colours tend to become hot when exposed to direct sunlight, which helps to accelerate the breakdown process.

Gloss retention can be improved significantly by the use of UV inhibitors, which absorb ultraviolet light before it does too much damage to the coating, although basic formulation is always the most important factor.

Modified resins

The alkyd resins used in conventional yacht coatings are usually manufactured from soya bean and linseed oils for a good balance of durability and performance at reasonable cost. Nevertheless, these properties can often be improved by incorporating other resins or oils, and by reaction with other monomers in a process known as *modifying*.

One of the most useful variants is the *urethane-modified alkyd*, in which an alkyd resin is partially reacted with isocyanate monomers similar to those used in polyurethane curing agents. In effect, the resin in a urethane alkyd is already partially cured, so drying times are shortened considerably, which can sometimes cause application difficulties in warm weather.

Urethane alkyds have better hardness and abrasion resistance than conventional alkyds, with greater resistance to chemicals and water, and higher initial gloss, although their long-term gloss retention is sometimes not quite as good.

Urethane oils provide a slightly different approach, where a vegetable oil (rather than an alkyd resin) is reacted with isocyanates. Urethane oil resins are very tough, with good resistance to chemicals and water immersion, and so are widely used in primers for timber and metalwork above the waterline. These resins are also used in DIY paints like Japlac, although their gloss retention is poor when used outdoors, and they tend to be rather too fast drying for painting large areas like yacht topsides.

Where cost is not an obstacle, a proportion of the soya and linseed oils can be replaced with more expensive tung oil, as in many of the more costly yacht varnishes. This technique combines the benefits of improved gloss, durability and water resistance with a very pleasant old-fashioned feel, although the addition of tung oil usually slows drying quite noticeably.

Another useful variant is the *silicone-modified alkyd*, which has recently seen major improvements. Some early silicone alkyds gained a bad reputation for adhesion and overcoating problems, but recent formulations like International's Toplac[2] and Epifanes Nautiforte have overcome these difficulties to provide a lasting high-gloss finish with excellent brush application properties. The finish and gloss retention of silicone alkyds can rival that of many two-component polyurethanes, albeit with lower abrasion resistance. Unfortunately, this technology can only be used in paints, as silicone alkyd resins do not produce clear films.

---

[2] Brightsides in the USA.

We have seen some of the ways in which the performance of conventional resins can be enhanced, although this usually adds considerably to the cost of raw materials. There are also many ways in which resins can be 'value engineered' to meet the pricing targets demanded by large supermarket and DIY chains. These can include substituting the more expensive oils with cheaper alternatives such as rapeseed oil, or by reducing the actual quantity of oil used in the resin to produce what is known as a *short or medium oil alkyd*. While these materials appear to offer good value for money, they are not as pleasing to apply as traditional yacht coatings, and will be unlikely to provide the same degree of protection.

Performance limitations of conventional resins

Whatever changes are made, alkyd resins are subject to a number of shortcomings, which pose severe restrictions on their use. These limitations are chiefly a result of the loosely bonded nature of alkyd polymers, which are vulnerable to being broken apart by alkali. This clearly limits their chemical resistance, but, less obviously, it also makes them unsuitable for underwater use on metal boats, as corrosion produces alkaline metal soaps that quickly destroy conventional coating schemes. This effect is known as *saponification*. These limitations apply to all conventional coatings, *including* yacht enamels and many of the general purpose red oxide primers sold for priming bare steel.

More generally, though, alkyds have poor resistance to long periods in water, and will start to soften and break down after only two or three days' immersion. This obviously makes them a poor choice for underwater protection, but any form of long-term exposure to water or moisture is likely to cause failure. Problems are commonly caused by wet ropes on deck, wet leaves, canvas covers, and even moisture trapped beneath flower pots! Exposure to motor fuels, strong spirits and cosmetic products (like after-shave lotions) can also cause damage, with the latter products often leaving tell-tale rings where they have been trapped beneath bottles and spray cans, etc.

The conventional drying mechanism itself also has its weaknesses, especially when coatings are applied too thickly, or overcoated too quickly. Under these circumstances, only the outer surface of the resin is able to release solvent or absorb oxygen, so it tends to dry with a layer of semi-liquid material trapped underneath it. This effect is most often seen on horizontal areas like decks and cabin soles, where it is easy (and very tempting) to apply far too much material, but it can also occur where the coating

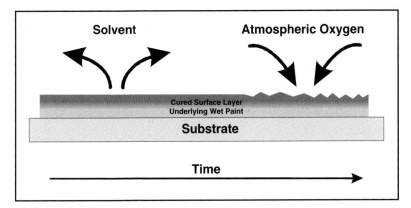

Fig 3 How excessive film thickness can cause drying problems. If conventional coatings are applied too thickly, only the outer surface will dry, trapping a layer of semi-liquid paint or varnish beneath it. As a rule of thumb, conventional paints and varnishes should be applied at no more than 100 μM (4 ml) wet film thickness if this effect is to be avoided. A photograph showing this effect can be seen on page 71.

runs to create small pools. In mild cases, the coating may appear inexplicably soft and easily damaged, but in severe cases wrinkling may occur as shown in Fig 3.

Failure of conventional coatings to *through dry* has become a common problem in recent years, owing to the removal of lead dryers from paints and varnishes. Although only used in tiny quantities, lead dryers were unsurpassed for promoting through drying, and have proved difficult to replace. Alternative dryers have been found, but it is worth noting that excessive application or premature overcoating is likely to cause difficulties, and should be avoided.

However, unlike most other drying mechanisms, the conventional drying process does not end when the coating has dried, but continues slowly throughout the life of the coating scheme. This results in gradual hardening of paint films, accompanied by gradual improvements in abrasion and chemical resistance which usually reach a peak after about four or five years. At this stage, many conventional paints are well enough cured to be overcoated with two-component polyurethanes, and can be quite difficult to remove with chemical paint strippers.

Unfortunately, this drying process produces by-products that are thought to contribute to the eventual embrittlement and breakdown of the coating. One interesting consequence is that many conventional coatings tend to yellow more if they are *not* exposed to sunlight, eventually becoming quite dull and brown in dark areas like lockers, cabins and galleys. This is because ultraviolet light breaks down the compounds responsible for yellowing, effectively bleaching the coating, but – as we have already seen – it does a lot of damage too. The dryers used to stimulate the drying process also tend to hasten this breakdown, so care is always taken to use only minimal amounts.

Conventional coatings will always play an important role in protecting yachts, but the need for better durability has led to the development of many new resin systems which use entirely different technology to provide practical benefits and greatly extended service life. Coatings manufactured from these resins are invariably more difficult to apply than conventional materials, and are usually more expensive, but their outstanding performance is finding an ever-increasing market within the yacht industry.

◆ TWO-COMPONENT EPOXIES

Marine epoxies are usually supplied as separate base and curing agents, which must be mixed together shortly before use. The mixed epoxy is then applied to the substrate while in liquid form, where it is converted into a solid, densely cross-linked polymer by chemical reaction. This process is entirely self-contained, and allows epoxies to be applied at much higher film thicknesses than is possible with conventional coatings.

Like polyurethanes, epoxies cure to produce a rigid three-dimensional molecular structure, with excellent mechanical and chemical properties; but while these two materials may appear outwardly similar, their chemistry and properties are quite different.

Epoxy polymer chains are comprised of only carbon-carbon and ether linkages, both of which are very stable; and bestow epoxies with their excellent chemical resistance, moisture barrier and electrical insulation properties. This combination of chemical and mechanical benefits, allied with good adhesive and penetrative qualities, has made epoxies an ideal choice for marine anticorrosive primers, yacht profiling fillers and adhesives such as Araldite®.

Where appropriate, these properties can be further improved by adding *lamellar* pigments like aluminium or mica flake for enhanced moisture barrier and anticorrosive properties. Epoxies may also be modified with coal tar to enhance their anticorrosive performance, although use in the yacht market has always been limited by their tendency to bleed when overcoated with light-coloured paints.

As would be expected, epoxies work well as underwater coatings, and most can also be used to protect substrates in demanding locations such as bilges, engine rooms and inside fuel tanks. Special epoxies are manufactured for potable water tanks, and are formulated to avoid the use of harmful raw materials like phenols or chromates, which could contaminate or taint drinking water.

However, the epoxy materials of greatest interest to the paint chemist are the low molecular weight variants, which are far more reactive and lower in viscosity than high molecular weight types. Low molecular weight resins have the benefit of requiring less solvent addition, and as the reactive groups are more mobile, they can usually be cured at lower temperatures.

Low viscosity also allows versatility in formulation, allowing the manufacture of totally solvent-free profiling fillers and laminating resins, as well as the solvent-free high build coatings used for osmosis treatment and specialist wood coatings. But unfortunately these highly reactive materials are severely irritating to the skin, and are known to cause dermatitis and other serious disorders by repeated skin contact. Some of the lower molecular weight epoxies are also volatile, causing irritation to the skin, eyes and respiratory tract if applied in confined spaces without adequate ventilation. Amine curing agents pose the greatest risk, although most are now reacted with some base resin during manufacture to cross link the most reactive (and harmful) groups, producing what is known as an *amine adduct*.

Nevertheless, whatever type of epoxy material is being used, skin contact must be avoided, and all work carried out in well-ventilated conditions. Further information on the safe use of epoxies can be found on page 125.

Performance limitations of epoxies

Despite their outstanding chemical and physical properties, epoxies still suffer from a number of practical limitations. The first is that epoxies have poor resistance to weathering, becoming very drab and chalky within just a few months of outdoor exposure. This is not a problem for underwater use or hidden areas, but where topsides and superstructures are being painted, it is customary to overcoat the epoxy with two component polyurethane undercoats and finishes for a lasting high-gloss finish. Conventional enamels may also be used, although their mechanical properties are comparatively poor. Furthermore, enamels have poor adhesion to epoxies unless the epoxy surface is thoroughly sanded and allowed to cure for a month or more before overcoating.

Curing conditions are also important: it is not generally appreciated that epoxies need warm, dry curing conditions if they are to reach a full state of cure, and are to provide optimum protection. While many epoxies will cure satisfactorily at temperatures down to 7 or 8° C (45 or 47° F), essential reactive groups within the resin become immobile at lower temperatures, bringing the curing reaction to a halt. Unfortunately, subsequent heating even to quite high temperatures will not re-start the curing process, and it may be necessary to remove the affected coatings if they are badly undercured.

A further problem involves the tendency of some epoxies to form a thin, sticky layer of amine carbomate on their outer surfaces while curing. Better known as amine sweating (or amine blushing), this phenomenon is caused by migration of amine curing agent to the coating surface, where it reacts with atmospheric moisture and carbon dioxide. Amine carbomate is water soluble (forming an alkaline solution), and is likely to cause blistering and detachment if not removed before overcoating.

Solvent-free coatings and fillers are most at risk from this problem, which is most likely to occur in cold, damp curing conditions where rate of cure is comparatively slow, giving the hygroscopic curing agent plenty of time to migrate. Warm, dry curing conditions help to minimise this tendency, and also improve curing.

Like polyurethanes, the solvents used in epoxies are rather more aggressive than ordinary white spirit, and are prone to softening conventional coatings. As a general rule, epoxies must not be applied over any coating that is unsuitable for underwater use; nor can they be used to protect or convert an otherwise unsuitable coating scheme.

◆ TWO-COMPONENT POLYURETHANES

Most true polyurethanes are supplied as two separate components, comprising a polyol base component and an isocyanate curing agent which must be mixed together shortly before the paint is applied. Once mixed, the two components react together to form a densely cross-linked, three-dimensional molecular structure, with outstanding resistance to ultraviolet degradation, mechanical damage and chemical attack.

The polyol base component is a type of polyester, which provides reactive hydroxyl (OH) sites with which the isocyanate curing agent can react. Polyols are manufactured from a wide range of raw materials, including some of those used to produce alkyd resins. The isocyanates are a family of nitrogen compounds existing in both aromatic and aliphatic forms, all containing the nitrogen=carbon=oxygen (N=C=O) isocyanate group.

Most early formulations were based upon the aromatic variant called *toluene diisocyanate* (TDI), but were very prone to premature yellowing and loss of gloss, although it must be said that TDI did provide a good degree of versatility in formulation. However, health concerns and the need to improve outdoor durability have meant that nearly all polyurethanes are now cured with the less reactive (and more expensive) aliphatic compound, *hexamethylene diisocyanate*.

In practical terms, polyurethanes will retain their finish for at least twice as long as conventional materials, and are far more resistant to the wear and tear of life on board. Polyurethanes also have excellent natural adhesion to well prepared gel coats, and are an obvious choice when choosing a scheme to rejuvenate old and faded glassfibre boats. They also work well when applied over epoxy anticorrosive schemes, although care is needed to avoid undercure caused by reaction with any residual solvent from the epoxy coatings. Moreover, the excellent resistance of polyurethanes to heat and chemical attack makes them an ideal choice for the galley and cabin, where they can last for 20 years or more and still look as good as new.

Polyurethanes are, however, comparatively impermeable to moisture, which can cause problems on some timber substrates. Furthermore, while fairly flexible in a bending sense, polyurethanes are not very elastic, and are usually considered unsuitable where movement or flexing is likely to occur. They are also more difficult to repair than conventional coatings, and so are less suitable in areas prone to mechanical damage.

Polyurethanes are *comparatively* tolerant to poor application conditions, and will cure reasonably well at temperatures down to 7 or 8° C (45 or 47° F), although their curing agents have a tendency to react with moisture in preference to the polyol base. This sometimes causes undercure in cold or damp environments, leading to soft films, poor gloss and, in extreme cases, gas bubbling within the paint film.

This moisture sensitivity is put to good use in single-component moisture-cured polyurethane wood primers such as Blakes Woodseal and International UCP.[3] Moisture-cured primers work extremely well on bare timber, penetrating deep into the grain where they can react with moisture in the wood fibres. These primers are easy to use, but should be applied thinly to prevent clouding caused by the tiny bubbles of carbon dioxide gas evolved while curing. Overcoating intervals must also be strictly observed if problems with intercoat adhesion are to be avoided.

[3] US Equivalent = Interprime wood sealer clear 102b.

A few moisture-cured undercoats and finishes are also available, although manufacturing difficulties mean that these are unlikely to become mass market products.

Unfortunately, the solvents used in polyurethane coatings are more aggressive than white spirit, and are prone to softening and wrinkling conventional coatings. Nevertheless, aged enamels can sometimes be overcoated to gain the cosmetic benefits of polyurethanes, although the mechanical properties of the scheme will only be as good as the weakest coat.

Performance limitations of polyurethanes

Two-component polyurethanes provide excellent cosmetic and mechanical performance in a wide variety of applications, but there are inevitably some restrictions. The main limitations are concerned with the moisture sensitivity of polyurethanes during cure, and can usually be avoided by painting in warm and dry conditions.

Care must also be taken at all stages to avoid contaminating the paint components and thinners with moisture. Polyurethane curing agents are especially prone to moisture absorption during storage, and must not be used if they have started to gel, or have discoloured beyond a pale straw shade.

Use of correct thinners in polyurethanes is also important: white spirit as used in conventional paints will cause flocculation or gelling, while epoxy thinners will cause undercure – and possibly gas bubbling owing to their alcohol content. Likewise, adequate overcoating intervals must be allowed when applying polyurethane finishing schemes over epoxies, as any residual alcohol may adversely affect cure.

While a well-cured polyurethane has an exceptionally hard surface, it should be remembered that the total film thickness of the finish is considerably less than that of a polyester gel coat, therefore any repeated abrasion will quickly wear through the coating scheme. Fender wear is the most common problem here, and can be largely avoided by replacing old and dirty fenders. New fenders should be washed occasionally with warm soapy water to remove sticky surface deposits that attract sand and grit. The use of fender socks can also be helpful.

Unfortunately, all polyurethane curing agents contain traces of free *isocyanate monomer*, a highly toxic material that can cause serious respiratory disorders if inhaled while spraying. To avoid this risk, full-face air-fed respirators *must* be worn when applying polyurethanes with a spray gun, and all other personnel evacuated from the area. (For further information, see Isocyanate Cured Polyurethane Paints and Varnishes on page 126)

Brush application is, however, quite safe provided that adequate ventilation is provided and good working practices are observed.

'Isocyanate free' polyurethane finishes have been in development for many years, but as yet, they do not provide the gloss or durability required for marine applications.

◆ OTHER TYPES OF RESIN

The resins that we have discussed so far are known as *converting* resins, because they undergo a permanent and irreversible chemical change on drying, and are not re-soluble in their original solvents. Converting coatings work well if they are applied in good drying conditions, but their performance can be very poor if applied under unfavourable conditions.

These drawbacks can often be overcome by using a *non-converting* resin system, which dries solely by solvent evaporation, and does not need to undergo any permanent chemical change. These are sometimes known as *lacquer drying coatings*. Cellulose paints are probably the best-known example, although these have limited uses today apart from minor car repairs, aerosol paints and nail varnishes.

In marine practice, chlorinated rubber paints and vinyl tars are the most widely used examples, and can provide excellent anticorrosive and moisture barrier properties provided that an adequate film thickness is applied. However, the abrasion resistance of these coatings is poor and, being non-converting, they are readily re-dissolved by their own solvents or by spillage of oils and fuels.

Cellulose paints have largely been replaced by acrylics; these provide much better performance, and can be used in both solvent and water-borne formulations. However, pure acrylic coatings have found few applications in the marine industry, as their resistance to abrasion and long-term water immersion is poor. A further drawback is that spray application and high temperature stoving is usually required to achieve a good cosmetic finish.

One useful variant is the acrylated polyurethane (technically known as a *hydroxyl branched acrylic*), which is cross-linked with isocyanate curing agents to enhance its mechanical and chemical properties. Examples like Awlgrip's Awlcraft 2000 are easy to apply by spray, and provide an exceptionally high-gloss finish, but are unsuitable for brush application except to very small areas.

Most of the resins and coatings that we have discussed so far require significant additions of organic solvents during their manufacture, which then evaporate shortly after application. Apart from the high cost of these wasted materials, organic solvent emissions are very polluting, and are associated with photochemical smog and other environmental problems that afflict our towns and cities.

Solvents can also pose severe health and fire hazards, so maximum effort is now being put into formulating solvent-free and reduced-solvent coatings. Indeed, in many countries legislation has been introduced to limit the percentage of these *volatile organic compounds* (or VOCs) present in paints, leading to the development of so-called 'VOC compliant' and 'high solids' coatings.

However, the ultimate goal is to eliminate organic solvents altogether wherever possible. Solvent-free epoxies are now widely used for both industrial and marine applications, and a few solvent-free polyurethanes are also available. Water-borne coatings are also becoming highly developed, where resins containing only a minimal amount of solvent are dispersed into water as an emulsion of tiny droplets. As the water evaporates, these droplets fuse together to form a continuous film which behaves in much the same way as usual solvent-borne coatings. Where necessary, the resin system can also be isolated (or blocked) from its aqueous base, so allowing the use of resin systems that would not usually tolerate moisture.

◆ PIGMENTS AND EXTENDERS

Pigments play an essential role in the formulation of paint coatings. Apart from the obvious benefit of providing colour and opacity, pigments significantly improve the adhesion and film strength of coatings. Pigments also play an important role in primers, where they are used to inhibit corrosion and to provide a barrier against moisture and oxygen. However, as the primary use for pigments is to provide colour, we shall look first at how they work in this role.

Visible light is comprised of electromagnetic energy having wavelengths between 0.4 to 0.7 μM. Violet light has the shortest wavelength at about 0.4 μM, followed by blue, green, yellow, orange and red light, which has a wavelength of about 0.62 μM. Wavelengths above and below these figures are not directly visible to the human eye, although they sometimes affect our perception of colours.

White pigments like titanium dioxide appear white because they reflect all colours (or wavelengths) of visible light more or less equally, while coloured pigments absorb light of some wavelengths while reflecting others, so all that we see is the reflected light. Black pigments absorb almost all visible light including infra-red, which is why black surfaces become very hot in direct sunlight.

Up until the late 1970s, lead and cadmium pigments were popular for their bright, strong colours and good resistance to fading, but these have now been replaced almost universally with organic pigments which are much safer in use. The opacity of these organic pigments is often poor, although they now have much better UV resistance (or lightfastness) than some early examples. Some organic pigments (notably toluidine red) are also quite soluble in organic solvents, and tend to bleed into lighter colours applied over them: this poses a particular problem when used in antifoulings. Other notable organic pigments include the phthalocyanine (or Monastral®) blues and greens with their characteristically strong, clean colours, which are widely used for tinting, and to produce deep shades like Oxford Blue and British Racing Green.

Where more subtle colorants are required, red or black iron oxides and yellow ochres are often used, either in their naturally occurring forms, or (more commonly now) synthetically manufactured. These do not have the clean colours or high tinting strengths of organic pigments, but they do provide much better opacity.

These are just a few examples, but in all there are literally hundreds of pigments available to the paint chemist, each having its own particular benefits, be it of colour, tinting strength, opacity, lightfastness, cost or availability. In practice, it is usually possible to manufacture any one colour with many different pigment combinations, but this often leads to problems when trying to match existing shades owing to an effect known as *metamerism* (see page 130). Where this occurs, paints may appear to match perfectly under one light source (ie daylight), but will appear markedly different under other lighting conditions. This creates a problem when trying to colour match one manufacturer's shade with another, or when trying to replicate the shade of polyester gel coats.

Fluorescent pigments are also worthy of mention because they convert ultraviolet light that we cannot see into visible light, which is why they appear to *fluoresce* or light up. Unfortunately, the chemical structure of many pigments (especially organics) is prone to being broken down by ultraviolet light, bringing about a permanent change in colour. This effect is better known as fading, and can be minimised by binding the pigment with a suitable resin, and by adding ultraviolet inhibitors to absorb the harmful rays before they do too much damage.

The ratio of pigment to binder in the dried paint, known as the *pigment volume concentration* (PVC), is also significant, and plays an important part in determining qualities like gloss, opacity and weather resistance. Paints with high PVCs are popular for household use owing to their good opacity and non-drip properties, although their gloss levels and weathering properties resistance are comparatively poor. Undercoats usually have the highest PVCs for optimum obliteration and sanding properties, and could almost be regarded as *underbound*.

Yacht finishes tend to have quite low PVCs, with more than adequate resin to completely surround each pigment particle. This sometimes means that several coats are required to achieve complete obliteration of the underlying colour, although gloss and weather resistance is much improved as a consequence.

The use of pigments in primers is particularly interesting: many primers formulated for metal substrates contain metallic pigments such as powdered zinc or aluminium flake, which provide localised sacrificial protection in the event of mechanical damage. Others contain pigments such as red iron oxide or zinc chromate, which provide good anticorrosive properties even when they are applied in thin films (as in holding primers).

Pigments with leaf or flake-like structures are particularly useful in primers, where they overlap like roof tiles to form an effective barrier against both moisture and oxygen (see Fig 5). These 'leafing', or lamellar, pigments are also used in barrier coats (see page 128) to reduce the

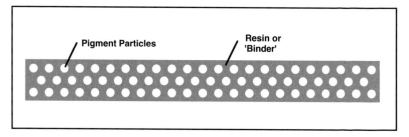

Fig 4 Cross-section of a well bound paint coating, showing how pigment particles are completely surrounded by resin.

absorption of aggressive solvents, and to reduce unsightly bleeding from coal tar coatings. Less obviously, the rather rough or granular surface finish produced by leafing pigments also improves intercoat adhesion, a property that is put to good use in some antifouling tie coats. In marine coatings, aluminium and mica flake are the most popular lamellar pigments, but some heavy-duty epoxy tank coatings use glass flake pigments to protect against exceptionally aggressive cargoes.

So far, we have discussed pigments that are used to provide colour, inhibit corrosion or provide barrier-like properties. However, there is another group of pigments known as *extenders*, which do not fit into any of these categories, but which nevertheless play an important role in coating formulation.

Many pigments would provide limited opacity (or hiding power) if used by themselves, and would be expensive if used in sufficient quantities to achieve complete obliteration. By using an extender like barytes (barium sulphate) or china clay, much smaller quantities of colouring pigment are needed, while opacity is improved. The largest quantities of extenders are used in undercoats, where long-term colour retention is not too important, but good opacity and ease of sanding is essential.

Another useful group of extenders are the thixotropes like silica powders and bentone clays, which are used to modify the body and feel of coatings. Small quantities of thixotropes are commonly used to improve application qualities and film build, and to help prevent settlement of pigments during storage. Larger quantities are used in the manufacture of non-drip paints, and in high-build epoxy primers where wet film thicknesses of 300 μ (0.012in) or more can be achieved without the risk of sagging. Silica powders can also be used as matting agents to reduce the gloss levels of varnishes and paint finishes.

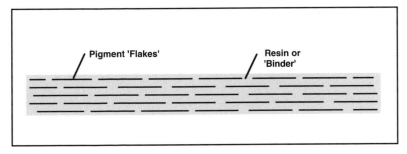

Fig 5 How leafing or lamellar pigments improve the barrier properties of coatings.

A rather different type of extender is used in the low-density profiling fillers used for filling and fairing yachts: the density of these fillers is all important, so a large amount of their volume is taken up by glass or polypropylene micro balloons which, being hollow, are very light in weight. Apart from minimising the total mass of the filled yacht, the very low density of these fillers allows application thicknesses of 2 centimetres (¾ inch) or more with little risk of the filler slumping under its own weight.

◆ SOLVENTS, DILUENTS AND THINNERS

In terms of paint formulation, solvents could be described as something of a necessary evil: they are expensive, they pose fire and health hazards, and they are associated with photochemical smog and other environmental problems. Nevertheless, without solvents, the manufacture and application of many paints could never take place.

Most of the resins used to make paints and varnishes are supplied either as very viscous, syrupy fluids, or as solids. These must be dissolved in solvents to reduce their viscosity so that pigments and extenders can be incorporated, and so that paint can be processed and filled into tins.

Once the paint has been manufactured, further solvent is often added by the end user in the form of a thinner or reducer, to adjust viscosity to suit the application method and conditions. By this stage, 75–80 per cent of the applied paint may be solvent, with only 20–25 per cent actual paint solids remaining.

As with pigments, there is a wide range of solvents available to the paint chemist, most of which are either extracted from crude oil or, less commonly now, from coal and wood processes. Solvents are classified by their chemical type (ie aromatic hydrocarbons, esters, ketones and alcohols), and also by their evaporation rates.

There would be little point in examining the significance of the different chemical types here, except to say that solvents are chosen for their ability to dissolve certain types of resin, and are therefore specific to certain types of coating. These are known as *true solvents* because a specified resin is infinitely soluble in them.

If a solvent of the wrong chemical type is used, the paint may gel, and could even fail to cure properly. Interestingly, though, many resins will tolerate limited amounts of an incompatible solvent, provided that a sufficient quantity of true solvent is also present. Solvents that can be used for thinning, but which are not true solvents, are known as *diluents*, and often provide better application characteristics than true solvents used alone.

Diluents are widely used in spray thinners for two-pack polyurethanes where a large degree of viscosity reduction is required, although care is needed in formulation to ensure that the diluent always evaporates before the true solvent. Likewise, some epoxies require separate thinners and equipment cleaners, because the thinner contains a large amount of diluent, and can only be tolerated in limited quantities.

The rate of solvent evaporation has a significant effect on application properties, and is an important factor in coating formulation. Spray thinners typically contain a mixture of five or six different solvents, the most volatile of which are used to help spray atomisation, although these usually evaporate before they reach the surface being painted. The slower evaporating solvents are used to promote flow, levelling and wet edge, and may take several hours (or even days) to evaporate completely. Unfortunately, volatile solvents absorb a great deal of heat as they evaporate, effectively refrigerating the applied paint. This tends to encourage moisture condensation when spraying in humid conditions, and may result in dulling or loss of gloss.

Much slower evaporating solvents are used in brushing thinners, and in high-temperature or 'tropical' spray thinners where flow and wet edge properties are important. Indeed, it is often possible to use a compatible brush thinner to *slow down* a spray product in hot weather, although it is always best to check with the manufacturer first.

◆ ADDITIVES

While additives account for only 3–4 per cent of a paint or varnish, they play a vital role in making it work. Some of the most important additives are the dryers used in conventional coatings to promote absorption of oxygen from the atmosphere. The actual quantity of dryers used varies from batch to batch, and is usually determined from drying tests carried out in the Quality Assurance Laboratory using a Drying Track Recorder. Excessive additions of dryers must be avoided, as they accelerate film ageing and promote solvent entrapment (see page 131).

Similar additives are used to adjust the rate of cure and pot lives (see page 130) of two-component polyurethanes, while the rate of cure of epoxies is usually inherent in their formulation, and can only be slightly altered by additives.

Ultraviolet absorbers are used in some coatings to absorb harmful ultraviolet rays before they can damage chemical bonds in the resin system to cause loss of gloss and chalking. Other additives can include silica matting agents to provide a satin finish, anti-skinning agents, flow and wetting agents, and special additives to help overcome manufacturing problems.

A limited number of these additives are made available to end users, usually to accelerate drying, or to overcome application problems such as cissing (see page 128). While some of these can prove useful in overcoming specific problems, it must be stressed that paint formulation is a very complex subject, and that no single additive can ever cure all ills. The use of silicone anti-cissing agents in particular demands extreme caution, for while small amounts can help to prevent cissing, excessive use will actually promote it. Moreover, any subsequent coats are even more likely to ciss, and their adhesion will be reduced.

◆ PAINT MANUFACTURE

When the work of formulation and testing has been completed, our paint is finally ready to be manufactured. The first stage in this process is to dissolve the resin into solvent to make what is basically a simple varnish; this may take several hours. The pigments and extenders are then stirred into a portion of the resin solution to make a slurry called a *mill base* or *grind charge* ready for the dispersion or 'grinding' stage.

The dispersion process itself is one of the most important stages in the whole manufacturing process, and plays a significant part in the quality and appearance of the applied paint. Paints made with well dispersed pigments provide far better colour and obliteration than poorly dispersed examples, and also have better gloss. The traditional way of doing this was to put the slurry into a *ball mill*, which is simply a very large steel drum lined with porcelain (or *Steatite*), and part filled with porcelain balls. As the drum is rotated, the balls rise up one side of the drum, and then cascade down the other side (rather like a large washing machine), dividing the pigment into smaller and smaller particles. The dispersion process continues for 16 hours or so, until the pigment particles have been reduced to a size of (typically) less than 5 μ when measured with a *grind gauge*. Ball milling has now largely been superseded by faster methods such as horizontal bead milling and high-speed dispersion, although the principles are much the same.

With the pigments dispersed, the slurry is 'let down' with the remainder of resin and solvent, and transferred to a large mixing tank. The batch is then tinted to the specified shade using concentrated pigment dispersions before samples are taken to the Quality Assurance Laboratory for batch testing.

Using these samples, test additions of solvent and additives like dryers are made to determine how much of each should be added to the batch to achieve correct viscosity and drying times. The sample is also tested for specific gravity to confirm that all ingredients have been added, and is applied to a piece of tinplate, glass, or special black and white test cards to check for correct colour, gloss, opacity and freedom from flocculation. Depending on the product, there may be other special tests, but it will be seen that nothing is left to chance.

When these tests have been completed, the batch is finally approved for filling off into tins, using special filters to remove any foreign matter. Final samples are also taken, and will be retained until there is little likelihood of the product remaining on chandlers' shelves.

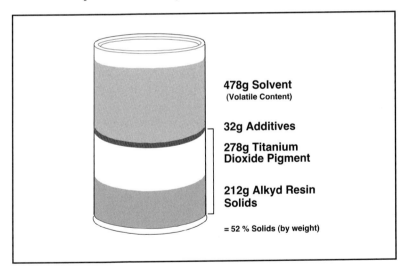

478g Solvent
(Volatile Content)

32g Additives

278g Titanium
Dioxide Pigment

212g Alkyd Resin
Solids

= 52 % Solids (by weight)

Fig 6 Constituents of a typical 750 ml can of white yacht enamel.

4 | Surface preparation

Now that we have a better idea of how paints are formulated and manufactured, we can take a closer look at how surfaces should be prepared before painting. Put simply, the aim of good surface preparation is to ensure maximum adhesion to the substrate, thereby maximising both the performance and the lifespan of the coating scheme. While preparation methods will vary depending on the substrate involved, the requirements are much the same:

- To provide a good mechanical key or anchor profile.
- To remove corrosion products (such as rust).
- To maximise chemical and mechanical adhesion by removing any surface oil, grease or wax.
- To remove any water soluble materials like sea salt and corrosion inhibitors.

◆ EXISTING PAINT SCHEMES

In most circumstances, paint will be applied over an existing coating scheme. Where this is the case, we must first make sure that the scheme is in sound condition, and that the old and new coatings will be compatible with each other.

Overcoating compatibility is often a worry when painting, but the ground rules are really quite simple: in general, high performance coatings (ie two-component epoxies and polyurethanes) can be overcoated with almost any type of paint, whereas conventional coatings, like yacht enamels, can only be overcoated with other single-component materials. This is simply because the solvents used in high performance coatings are very aggressive, and they tend to attack conventional coatings, causing softening and wrinkling.

There are, nevertheless, occasions where aged enamels in sound condition can be successfully overcoated with two-component finishes, although this can never be guaranteed. Conversely, it should be noted that adhesion of conventional coatings to two-component materials tends to be poor unless the surface is very well prepared; this is partly because there is no chemical bond between the coatings, and because the comparatively mild solvent used in conventional coatings (ie white spirit) has little softening effect on epoxies and polyurethanes.

However, our first task should be to examine the existing paint scheme, and to ascertain whether it can be overcoated successfully. Painting schemes can last for many years, but remember that the very first coat will be the oldest, and that any paint scheme can only be as good as its weakest coat.

Examine the scheme closely for any signs of blistering or peeling, investigating any suspicious lumps or bumps with a sharp wood chisel or a penknife. Breakdown will usually be most evident around sharp edges, where coatings tend to peel away from the substrate, or from each other. Localised detachment is not necessarily a problem, but if the coatings can be picked up and peeled away, total removal may need to be considered before repainting.

If there is any doubt about the integrity of the scheme, it is worth carrying out a simple adhesion test. To do this, a series of deep cuts are made in the paint scheme with a scalpel or very sharp knife, using a cross-hatched pattern as shown in Fig 7.

When the cuts have been made, the surface should be wiped with a clean dry cloth to remove any loose cuttings, and a piece of adhesive tape (such as Sellotape®) stuck firmly on to the paint. The tape is then tugged sharply upwards, and a count taken of the number of squares removed.

If the test area remains mostly intact, overcoating should present no problems, but if more than about 10 per cent of the squares are removed, either the entire paint scheme or at least the poorly adherent coatings will need to be removed before repainting.

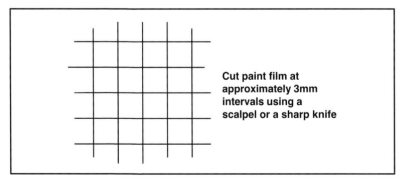

Cut paint film at approximately 3mm intervals using a scalpel or a sharp knife

Fig 7 Preparing for an adhesion test.

Having confirmed that the existing coatings are sound, the next task will be to decide on a suitable painting scheme. Application of conventional coatings should present few problems, but if high performance (two-pack) coatings are to be applied, compatibility will need to be checked first. Where it is certain that a two-component system was previously applied, it will be quite safe to apply further high performance coatings, but if the history of the scheme is unknown, a simple compatibility test should be carried out.

This is done by wetting a clean white cotton cloth with polyurethane spray thinner or nail varnish remover, and gently rubbing the suspect coating for 10 minutes or so. If the coating shows any signs of softening or wrinkling, or if the cloth becomes strongly discoloured by the paint, overcoating with a two-component material is likely to cause similar problems. However, if no adverse effects are observed, it should be safe to apply two-component materials.

The final cautions concern the condition of the substrate itself. Metal yachts must be inspected closely to ensure that no corrosion is present under the paintwork, as metals corrode very rapidly in confined spaces, sustaining severe damage within quite a short time. Aluminium is especially prone to this problem, being quickly destroyed by its own corrosion salts. Unfortunately, the powdery white aluminium hydroxide appears to be quite harmless, and often goes unnoticed until a great deal of damage has already been done.

Steel can also suffer quite severe corrosion under paint schemes, although fortunately this is usually evident by tell-tale rust staining. If any corrosion is found, the coatings must be removed locally, and the metal thoroughly prepared before re-priming.

Having satisfied ourselves that the coating scheme is in sound condition, and is suitable for overcoating with our chosen painting scheme, preparation work can start in earnest.

◆ PREPARATION

The first task is to remove all surface contamination *before* sanding. This is important, because surface contamination is far more difficult to see and remove once the substrate has been roughened. This procedure is described in more detail in the section entitled Cleaning and Degreasing on page 58.

When degreasing has been completed, mechanical preparation can begin using 'wet or dry' abrasive paper. Where protective coatings are to be applied (ie underwater), the surface should be sanded with 80 or 120 grit paper to provide the best possible mechanical adhesion. However, if cosmetic coatings are to be applied (ie on topsides and superstructures), 180 or 220 grit paper should be used initially, followed by finer grades of up to 400 grit to prevent the sanding marks from showing through to the finish. In all cases, surfaces must be sanded with a firm, circular action until they are uniformly dull, with no glossy areas remaining; simply scratching the surface is of little benefit, and will not provide an adequate key for good coating adhesion.

Any damage should also be repaired at this stage by priming and filling as appropriate: if damage has penetrated the coating scheme, the surrounding area will need to be 'feathered back' using coarse sanding paper followed by localised priming. In the case of aluminium, thorough mechanical preparation is preferable to the use of etch primers, which must only be applied to completely bare metal.

When one or two coats of primer have been applied, an epoxy filler may be required to restore the original surface profile. A piece of stiff card (like a postcard) is often found useful for localised filling, and can easily be flexed to the desired shape. Avoid over-filling, as it will be hard work to sand off the excess filler, and there will be a greater risk of damage to surrounding areas. When filling work is completed, the patches of filler should be primed, undercoated (if appropriate), and then sanded smooth before the whole area is painted.

If the existing finish is in good condition, but has simply become dulled with age, it is usually possible to re-finish with just two or three coats of gloss finish, provided that a colour change is not required. In other cases, two or more coats of undercoat may be required to obliterate the colour, and to provide a smooth surface for finishing coats. These should be applied as outlined on pages 82 and 85.

If masking is required, a professional masking tape like 3M's Fineline™ will be found much easier to use than ordinary paper tapes. Fineline™ is made from a special plastic, which conforms well to curved or complex surfaces, and uses an adhesive that is not dissolved by solvents, so helping to avoid ragged edges. The tape is available in several different widths, and is sold widely by yacht chandlers and auto factors.

For most work, fresh masking tape should be applied for each coat; if the tape is left for too long, it can be difficult to remove, and may also tear away the edge of the fresh paint. Tapes are best removed by pulling them slowly at 90° from the surface when the paint has become just touch dry to avoid sharp, raised edges and 'strings' of slightly wet paint.

◆ GLASSFIBRE

From a painting point of view, glassfibre shares many similarities with two-component paint coatings, although there are some special considerations.

New gel coat has a very hard, glossy appearance, and will usually be contaminated with some mold release wax from manufacture. This wax is used to prevent the gel coat from sticking to the mold, and likewise it will prevent adhesion of paint coatings.

Like paint finishes, gel coats become very dull and faded with prolonged exposure to the elements, their surfaces eventually becoming chalky and difficult to clean. While their appearance can sometimes be restored by polishing, any benefits are usually short lived, with painting required to achieve any long-term improvement. Gel coats also tend to be very brittle, with a tendency to craze and crack if subject to stress or mechanical impact. In addition, some gel coats have many thousands of tiny air bubbles trapped in them, which become visible as pinholes when the surface is sanded. These defects can be difficult and time consuming to overcome, and should always be assessed before starting work.

Two-component polyurethanes are the best choice for re-finishing, providing gloss and abrasion resistance that is often better than the original gel coat. They also achieve excellent adhesion to gel coats by reacting with redundant chemical groups in the gel coat resin.

Conventional enamels can also provide good appearance (especially the silicone modified types), but they have little affinity for gel coats, and must only be applied to well prepared surfaces if they are to have good adhesion.

However, two points concerning abrasion resistance must be raised here: first, the abrasion resistance of conventional coatings is quite poor when compared to either polyurethanes or the original gel coat, and they can quickly become scratched and scuffed by mechanical damage or dirty fenders; secondly, paint films are very much thinner than gel coats, so any deep scoring is likely to penetrate the coating scheme, revealing the underlying colour.

Choosing a new finish with a similar colour to the original, or even using a similarly coloured undercoat will help to reduce this problem, but nevertheless it must be realised that paint coatings are comparatively thin, and must be given some care if they are not to be spoiled prematurely.

Preparation

As with all surface preparation, the first step is to remove any oil, grease or wax with a good degreaser. This procedure is described in more detail in the section entitled Cleaning and Degreasing on page 58, although it should be noted that acetone and strongly alkaline degreasers (ie caustic soda) must not be used on glassfibre.

When degreasing has been completed, surfaces should be thoroughly sanded with 'wet or dry' abrasive paper, used wet, to provide a good mechanical key. If protective coatings are to be applied (ie underwater), surfaces should be sanded with 80 or 120 grit paper to ensure good adhesion. However, where finish coatings are to be applied (ie on topsides and superstructures), 180 or 220 grit paper should be used initially, followed by finer grades of up to 400 grit to prevent sanding marks from showing through to the finish.

In all cases, surfaces must be sanded with a firm, circular action until they are uniformly dull, with no glossy areas remaining; simply scratching the surface is of little benefit, and will not provide an adequate key for good coating adhesion.

Any star crazing will need to be repaired at this stage, preferably by grinding out and then filling the affected area. Some painters prefer to deepen and widen each crack individually with a sharp tool, so that it forms a vee, but this is slow work, and is only practical when repairing localised damage. When doing this work, make sure that the crazed gel coat is well attached to the laminate, and is not loose, as it could quickly spoil the new finish.

Pinholing can be even more difficult to overcome, and is often not visible until after the first coat of paint has been applied. Large pinholes are best filled individually with a fine filler, which should be pressed well into the holes with a filling knife, although the filler can sometimes pop out again if any air is trapped. Smaller pinholes are virtually impossible to pack with filler, but they can usually be filled by brush applying two or three coats of undercoat, working each coat well into the surface. Spray application is not recommended, as the changing air pressure usually makes the paint pop out of the holes shortly after painting.

Underwater preparation is rather more straightforward, although we should always be aware of physical defects that can allow ready moisture ingress. Antifoulings must first be removed by wet sanding, or with a proprietary antifouling remover. *Do not* remove antifoulings by dry sanding or by burning because they contain toxic materials.

In practice it will often be found difficult to remove the colour staining from antifoulings, but this does not pose a problem as long as the antifoulings themselves have been completely removed. Any antifouling remaining in deep scratch marks can be removed with an antifouling remover, or with cloths soaked in a strong solvent (such as a polyurethane thinner). Advice on suitable masking tapes for this can be found on page 29.

What about osmosis?

Osmosis (also known as 'boat pox') can affect glassfibre laminates both above and below the waterline, and can affect any glassfibre yacht over two or three years old. But what is osmosis, and why is it so important?

Osmosis is caused by small amounts of moisture that permeate into the laminate, where they liberate tiny quantities of '*hygroscopic solutes*' over a prolonged period. We tend to think of osmosis as an underwater problem, although topsides and superstructures are just as prone to absorb moisture from wet canvas covers, wet ropes and even wet leaves on deck. Decks and coachroofs can also develop problems owing to rainfall and general exposure to the elements over many years.

Initially this moisture does little damage, and most of it passes harmlessly through the glassfibre and into the bilges, where it disperses as water vapour. Eventually though, the incoming moisture starts to break down (or hydrolyse) some of the raw materials used to manufacture the laminate. The main offenders here are propylene and ethylene glycols, which are often added to freshly cooked batches of polyester resin as 'moisture scavengers'. These should be completely removed before the resin is filled out into drums, but small quantities sometimes remain, and can result in premature blistering. Acetic and hydrochloric acids (liberated from some glass reinforcements) can cause similar problems, although this weakness has been largely overcome in boats built since the early 1990s.

As this circle of moisture absorption and laminate breakdown progresses, the volume of breakdown solutions within the laminate gradually increases, but as these solutions have a much larger molecular weight (or dimension) than moisture (H_2O), they are unable to escape back through the gel coat. This osmotic effect can ultimately result in gel coat blistering owing to hydraulic pressure generated within the laminate, although this is a very slow process, and it usually takes many years for the first blisters to develop. Fig 8 shows how this process evolves. So, in summary, osmosis could be defined as *chemical breakdown within a laminate owing to moisture ingress, which ultimately results in blistering of the gel coat.*

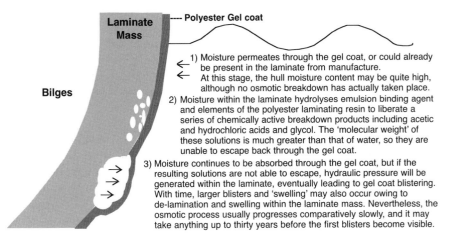

Fig 8 The osmotic process in glassfibre hulls.

Unfortunately, all paint coatings are slightly permeable to moisture, so once this breakdown process has started, painting alone will not halt it. And, more significantly, the paint scheme itself is likely to develop blisters within a season or two if osmotic breakdown products are trapped within the laminate.

Paint film blistering of this type is generally associated with underwater areas, though many yachts have suffered problems above the waterline where cosmetic finishing schemes have been applied. This is most likely to occur if the total film thickness of the painting scheme is inadequate, but this is not always the case. So what precautions should be taken before painting glassfibre?

First of all, the laminate should be checked with a good moisture meter to see whether it has a high moisture content. If the moisture content is low, it can usually be assumed that the laminate is in sound condition, and can be painted satisfactorily. Higher readings can be expected on underwater areas for a week or two after lifting, but these should fall steadily if the laminate is sound.

Persistently high moisture readings above or below the waterline should ring alarm bells: these indicate that some laminate breakdown has already occurred, and will not be reversed by painting, or by trying to force dry the laminate. Where these symptoms affect underwater areas, painting would not generally be advised, although it will not cause any damage so long as the risk of paint film blistering is understood and accepted.

Characteristic blistering of glassfibre gel coat caused by osmosis. This is a very slow process, and it may take up to 30 years for the first blisters to appear.

Regular checks with an electronic moisture meter will help to detect osmotic problems well before the first blisters appear. However, early treatment is rarely beneficial.

Similar advice applies to above-water areas, although increasing the total thickness of the painting scheme will help to delay any blistering by slowing down further moisture ingress. While it is difficult to give specific recommendations, I would advise that an absolute minimum of two coats of undercoat, and two coats of finish, are applied, giving a total dry film thickness in the order of 200 μ. Where possible, thicker schemes should be applied by using additional coats of undercoat before any finishing coats are applied: in this respect, International Paints recommend several coats of their Polyurethane Undercoat[4], while Awlgrip recommend several coats of their 545 epoxy primer.

◆ STEEL

Preparation of steel is quite straightforward, but must be thorough if the full benefit of high performance coating schemes is to be realised. New steels used for boatbuilding are supplied with a variety of surface treatments, although their basic properties are similar. The main exception to this rule is Corten, an alloy of iron, copper, chromium and nickel, which forms a tightly adherent protective rust layer to prevent metal loss. Corten is mainly used to fabricate shipping containers, and in architectural steelwork, where it does not need to be painted. However, for our purposes Corten

[4] Interprime 850 epoxy in the USA.

should be prepared and coated in exactly the same way as ordinary steels.

Most commercial vessels and large yachts are built using pre-primed steel plate, which is blasted with steel shot and then primed with a special *shop primer* at the steelworks. The shot-blasting process removes all mill scale from the steel, and avoids a great deal of work and expense during new building. The shop primer is designed to protect the steel during transport, storage and construction, and will usually be formulated (and certified) to allow welding without detriment to weld strength.

Many shop primers can be overcoated with full coating schemes, but if their age and history is uncertain, they should be removed by sweep blasting (ie a light grit blast), or abrasive discing when building work is completed, and an epoxy *holding primer* applied.

Some lighter gauge 'bright' steels are delivered with a coating of oil or grease to protect them from corrosion, which must be completely removed by degreasing before any other preparation work is started.

'Black steel' is the most difficult to prepare, owing to the very hard layer of mill scale on its surface. This oxide layer is formed while the white-hot steel ingots are being rolled into plates, and is very brittle. The mill scale tends to crack as the ingots cool, and if not removed may trap moisture, creating a strongly corrosive cell. The black oxide layer formed around welds has similar properties, and likewise can promote serious corrosion. Black steel is chosen by many small boatyards and DIY boatbuilders on the grounds of cost, although the work involved in preparation can far outweigh any initial savings.

Some boatbuilders prepare black steel by weathering, allowing it to rust so that the mill scale can be more easily removed by discing or wire brushing. This method has some validity, although in practice the standard of preparation achieved is very poor, and is certainly inadequate for high performance coating schemes.

Abrasive discing is an acceptable alternative, and is becoming increasingly popular owing to environmental restrictions; although the very hard nature of mill scale makes this technique slow and expensive except for small areas (ie around welds). Moreover, discing is of limited use where the metal is heavily pitted.

Rotary wire brushing is of little use as it tends to burnish the surface, and does not remove mill scale or firmly adhering rust. Acid pickling methods are used in some industrial preparation processes, but environmental and safety considerations make these inadvisable for general boatyard use.

Abrasive grit blasting is the only practical and effective method for preparing large areas of steel, and provides by far the best surface preparation standards. When properly carried out, grit blasting removes all mill scale and corrosion products, and provides an excellent anchor profile to ensure good coating adhesion. In this respect, it should be noted that grit blasting increases the effective surface area of metals by approximately 40–50 per cent, which significantly increases the adhesion of priming schemes.

The type and grade of abrasive grit chosen for blasting is also important, as it determines both production rates and the standard of preparation achieved. Black copper slag expendable abrasives (such as Jblast®)[5] are the most widely used for steel preparation, and can produce an excellent standard of preparation quickly and cost effectively. The use of very coarse grades of grit (as used for industrial steelwork) should be avoided, as they cause unnecessary damage to the metal, and produce an excessive surface profile which is difficult to paint satisfactorily. Moreover, blasting with coarse grit is also likely to distort flat plates, especially if these are of light gauge.

The use of sand, granite and other silicaceous abrasives is considered dangerous, and is prohibited in most developed countries owing to the health risks caused by the release of free silica.

Experience has shown that a well applied paint scheme provides the best and most cost effective protection for steel: the use of zinc or aluminium spraying techniques is not recommended, because, apart from high initial cost, the sprayed metal can be difficult to paint. Furthermore, these metals seriously limit the choice of antifouling, and can be difficult to re-coat when damaged or after re-blasting. Where additional protection is required, application of an additional coat(s) of epoxy and installation of comprehensive *cathodic protection* is usually preferable to other methods.

Initial preparation

Where new steel is to be painted, it is good practice to first grind smooth any welded seams and other protrusions, as paint tends to run away from sharp edges, resulting in thin coatings and reduced protection. Likewise, all weld spatter should be removed, as it will be almost impossible to coat evenly, and is often loosely adherent. These measures will improve the performance of the coating scheme, and will reduce the amount of filling and fairing required.

---

[5] Jblast® is manufactured by Wolverhampton Abrasive in the UK. Similar products are available elsewhere in the world including Black Beauty in the USA.

Once smooth, the bare steel must be thoroughly degreased to remove all cutting oils and other surface contamination before starting any other preparation work. This procedure is described in more detail in the section entitled Cleaning and Degreasing on page 58. Once degreased, prepared surfaces must not be touched by hand until painted in order to avoid grease spots and possible paint detachment. When degreasing has been completed, mechanical preparation work can begin.

Steel must only be prepared in dry conditions, and then only when the metal is at least 4° C or 7° F *above* the dew point temperature (see page 110 and 129) to avoid the risk of surface condensation. After preparation, the bare metal should be vacuum cleaned, and then primed with an epoxy holding primer within two or three hours to avoid *flash rusting* (p 129). Conventional primers can be used above water, but will fail if used to protect underwater areas. (Note that it is not possible to overcoat these primers with epoxies later.) However, in damp or humid conditions it may be necessary to apply the primer more quickly, although care must be taken to avoid contaminating the freshly applied paint with blasting grit, as this will promote corrosion.

Steel may be prepared by wet or dry grit blasting, although the latter method is usually favoured for marine applications unless the metal is heavily corroded or pitted. Wet blasting provides some benefits here, as the fresh water helps to remove soluble corrosion salts and reduces airborne dust concentrations, but it also causes flash rusting (see page 129). Where heavily corroded steel is dry blasted, high pressure washing at intervals during preparation will help to remove soluble corrosion salts: however, if beads of yellow fluid form on the steel after preparation, this indicates that some corrosion products are still present, and further preparation is required. If this problem is not treated before painting, further corrosion and failure of the coating scheme will almost certainly occur.

Corrosion inhibitors are sometimes added to water during washing or blasting to prevent flash rusting, but these *must not* be used on areas that will be immersed. This is because the inhibitors themselves are water soluble, and given time they will separate the coating scheme from the substrate. If a corrosion inhibitor has been used, the surfaces concerned *must* be thoroughly high pressure washed with fresh water in order to remove any soluble matter, and then dry sweep blasted to remove flash rusting.

Description	Swedish Standards Organisation (SIS 05.5900)	British Standards Council (BS 4232)	US Steel Structures Painting Council (SSPC)	US National Association of Corrosion Engineers (NACE)
White metal	Sa 3	First quality	SSPC - SP5	NACE No 1
Near white metal	Sa 2$^1/_2$	Second quality	SSPC - SP10	NACE No 2
Commercial blast	Sa 2	Third quality	SSPC - SP6	NACE No 3
Brush off blast	Sa 1	No standard	SSPC - SP7	NACE No 4

Fig 9 Steel preparation standards.

Fig 10 Blast cleaning to white metal standard (Sa 3).

Definition: Sa 3 – Blast cleaning to white metal
The blasting jet is passed over the surface long enough to remove all mill scale, rust and foreign matter. After blasting, the surface must be cleaned with a vacuum cleaner, dry compressed air or a clean brush. When prepared, the surface should have a uniform metallic colour.

Applications: Sa 3 is the best standard of preparation, and is recommended wherever high performance (ie epoxy) yacht coatings are to be applied.

Fig 11   Steel prepared to commercial blast standard (Sa 2).

Definition: Sa 2 – Thorough blast cleaning standard
The blasting jet is passed over the surface long enough to remove almost all mill scale, rust and foreign matter. After blasting, the surface must be cleaned with a vacuum cleaner, dry compressed air or a clean brush. When prepared, the surface should appear greyish in colour.

Applications: This preparation standard is suitable where conventional coatings are to be applied to yachts, and is generally acceptable where surface tolerant high performance protective coatings (ie epoxy tars) are to be applied to commercial vessels.

Steel preparation standards

The widespread use of steel in shipbuilding and civil engineering has led to several worldwide surface preparation standards being established. The best known are the Swedish steel preparation standards, where Sa 0 refers to unprepared (rusty) steel, and Sa 3 refers to white metal. A series of intermediate references (ie Sa 2 and Sa 2½) denote standards in between. A table of the most widely used standards is given in Fig 9, followed by descriptions and photographs of standards from Sa 1 to Sa 3 (Figs 10–12). (Note that all samples were blast cleaned with JBlast® abrasive media, using dry blasting apparatus.)

Fig 12   Steel brush off blast prepared (Sa 1).

Definition: Sa 1 Light blast cleaning standard
The (blasting) jet is passed rapidly over the surface so that loose mill scale, rust and foreign matter are removed.

Applications: This preparation standard would be considered unsatisfactory for most yacht coatings, but may be adequate for some commercial applications where approved by the paint manufacturer.

Initial priming of steel

When preparation work has been completed, all cleaning debris must be removed before painting: embedded dirt, grit or fragments of metal will promote rapid corrosion, and will reduce the protection provided by the painting scheme. Vertical surfaces may be cleaned by brushing or by dusting off with clean compressed air, although vacuum cleaning is a safer and more effective method, especially in tanks and bilges.

If there is any suspicion that blasting debris has not been completely removed, a piece of clear adhesive tape should be affixed to the surface, removed, and then examined closely for any signs of dust or grit: if the tape is contaminated, further cleaning is essential.

Once cleaned, the prepared steel should be primed with a suitable holding primer to prevent surface rusting, and to provide a basis for the complete coating scheme. Where possible, a holding primer should be applied within a few hours of blasting, especially in damp or humid conditions. On larger vessels, it may be necessary to establish a working pattern to avoid blasting near to freshly applied holding primer, thereby avoiding the risk of damaging or embedding grit in the new coating. Epoxy priming schemes are usually the first choice for priming steel both above and below the waterline, and can incorporate epoxy profiling fillers if required. Alternatively, chlorinated rubber or vinyl primers can be used below the waterline, while conventional primers can be used above.

Further information concerning the application of holding primers can be found on page 73.

◆ ALUMINIUM ALLOY

Aluminium offers many practical advantages as a boatbuilding material, being strong, lightweight, and quite easy to fabricate, although from a chemical viewpoint it is a highly reactive metal, and will readily corrode in a marine environment if not adequately protected.

In dry conditions, aluminium protects itself by forming a very thin, and almost invisible, oxide layer whenever it is cut, welded or sanded, but where there is insufficient oxygen for this layer to form, very rapid corrosion can occur. This problem is most prevalent in confined spaces such as cracks and crevices and behind poorly adherent paint films; although corrosive environments such as sewage holding tanks can also cause problems.

Unfortunately, the by-products of aluminium corrosion are themselves highly corrosive, and may cause serious pitting if trapped.

Clearly, this is a case where a badly applied paint scheme is worse than no paint scheme at all, so it is essential that great care is taken when preparing surfaces for painting, and that a suitable coating scheme is chosen. It is also important that any corrosion is treated at the earliest opportunity to avoid serious damage and costly repairs (see page 95).

Unfortunately, the protective oxide layer which forms on aluminium also makes the metal difficult to paint, as few coatings have more than marginal adhesion to it. To overcome this problem, three methods of preparation have evolved, namely abrasive *blast cleaning, abrasive discing* and *chemical preparation*. The first two methods work by providing a mechanical key, while the third uses chemical means to etch the oxide layer.

Where practicable, abrasive blast cleaning is usually the first choice, as it provides the best anchor profile for the coating scheme, while increasing the effective surface area by around 50 per cent. Blast cleaning is fast, and is also effective where corrosion has caused pitting, but it can cause distortion of thin metals if used too aggressively.

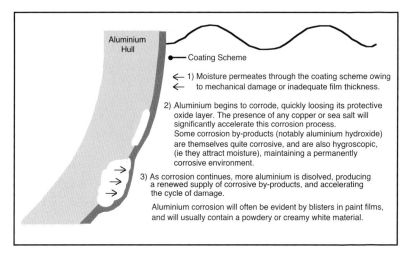

Aluminium
Hull

Coating Scheme

1) Moisture permeates through the coating scheme owing
to mechanical damage or inadequate film thickness.

2) Aluminium begins to corrode, quickly loosing its protective
oxide layer. The presence of any copper or sea salt will
significantly accelerate this corrosion process.
Some corrosion by-products (notably aluminium hydroxide)
are themselves quite corrosive, and are also hygroscopic,
(ie they attract moisture), maintaining a permanently
corrosive environment.

3) As corrosion continues, more aluminium is disolved, producing
a renewed supply of corrosive by-products, and accelerating
the cycle of damage.

Aluminium corrosion will often be evident by blisters in paint films,
and will usually contain a powdery or creamy white material.

Fig 13 The aluminium corrosion process.

While blast cleaning is an ideal option, this method is impractical (or even prohibited) in many areas, therefore alternative mechanical preparation methods are required. The most effective of these is abrasive discing, where very coarse (24 or 36 grit) sanding discs are used to heavily score the metal surface. Abrasive discing is widely used by many luxury yacht boatbuilders throughout Europe, and given correct use can provide perfectly good adhesion, although it is not as effective as grit blasting when preparing pitted metal and complicated surfaces. As with blast cleaning, an adequate surface profile is essential to ensure good coating adhesion.

Of the chemical preparation methods available for aluminium, self-etching primers are the most widely used. Most of these contain phosphoric acid, which reacts with the oxide layer to promote good chemical adhesion.

Sadly, etch primers are now largely obsolete in the marine industry, as the enforced removal of chromate pigments (which are toxic) has resulted in a significant loss of performance. Accordingly, the paint manufacturers now recommend that, wherever possible, all metals should be prepared by blast cleaning or abrasive discing as outlined previously. (Also see page 71.)

Where self-etch primers are available, these must be applied thinly to avoid failure by 'splitting'. Temperature is also important, as the etching process will fail if the *metal* (rather than the ambient) temperature falls

Fig 14 A badly corroded Mercruiser aluminium outdrive. Aluminium is very prone to corrosion and will quickly sustain expensive damage.

below 10° C/50° F. Successful etching is usually indicated by a noticeable change in colour within half an hour or so of application.

Care must also be exercised when overcoating with anti-corrosive primers, as excessively thick films can remain rich in solvent for some days, and once again will promote splitting.

The final caution concerns use in potable water tanks as some etch primers still contain chromate pigments that are known to be harmful to humans when dissolved in drinking water. While etch primers are usually overcoated, damage to or breakdown of the coating scheme may well expose the primer: so while etch primers can be safely used in sewage or fuel tanks, their use in freshwater tanks must be avoided.

Other chemical processes for preparing aluminium are available, chiefly from the aircraft industry. But while effective, these are often complex, and use chemicals that are hazardous for large scale use outside of a factory environment. These methods are also subject to increasing environmental pressure, and will not be considered further here.

Given the potential problems of chemical preparation methods, it will be seen that thorough mechanical preparation and the use of an epoxy holding primer is to be preferred wherever possible.

Initial preparation

Where new aluminium is to be painted, it is good practice to first grind smooth any welded seams and other protrusions, as paint tends to run away from sharp edges, resulting in thin coatings and reduced protection. Likewise, all weld spatter should be removed, as this is almost impossible to coat evenly, and is often loosely adherent. These measures will improve the performance of the coating scheme, and will reduce the amount of filling and fairing required later on.

Once smooth, the bare aluminium must be thoroughly degreased to remove all cutting oils and other surface contamination before starting any other preparation work. This procedure is described in more detail in the section entitled Cleaning and Degreasing on page 58; although it should be noted that strongly alkaline industrial degreasers containing sodium hydroxide (caustic soda) must not be used on any light alloys, as they are likely to damage the metal.

It is also essential to remove all traces of degreaser by thorough fresh water washing before any mechanical preparation is started, since any soluble material could separate the coating scheme from the substrate.

Once degreased, aluminium should be prepared and painted as quickly as possible to minimise surface contamination. Avoid touching the prepared surfaces until painted to avoid grease spots and possible paint detachment.

Mechanical preparation procedures

Where possible, aluminium should be prepared by dry abrasive blast cleaning, using aluminium oxide grit; this method provides the best surface profile for good paint adhesion, and quickly removes any surface corrosion deposits. Blast cleaning is also an effective method for preparing previously painted aluminium.

Prepared aluminium should appear uniformly light grey to white in colour, with a clearly discernible surface profile. As a guide, this will appear similar to steel prepared to 'White Metal Standard' (see Fig 10 on page 38), but will have a 'tighter' surface texture.

While aluminium oxide grit is expensive, it can be re-used several times without reducing the standard of surface preparation. Sand, granite and other siliceous abrasives must not be used as they liberate free silica when shattered, and in any case are rarely sharp enough to provide an adequate surface profile. Likewise, the use of black mineral slag abrasives (as used on steel) must also be avoided, as traces of metallic iron and copper embedded in aluminium will result in serious corrosion.

In situations where grit blasting is impractical (or prohibited), abrasive discing may be used as an alternative. A very coarse abrasive disc (24 or 36 grit) should be used to heavily score the surface, taking care to thoroughly roughen the entire area to be painted.

Whether aluminium is prepared by blasting or discing, a minimum surface profile of at least 50–75 μ must be achieved to ensure good coating adhesion. Ideally this should be measured with a surface profile gauge, but a close visual inspection will show whether or not the profile is satisfactory: if it is not, a single coat of etch primer must be applied prior to the holding primer.

If the surface profile is satisfactory, a single coat of an epoxy holding primer must be applied as quickly as possible, and preferably within six to eight hours of preparation. If the metal changes to a dull grey colour or becomes contaminated, the area must be degreased and prepared again before repainting.

There will of course be situations where extensive mechanical preparation cannot be carried out. In these cases, an etching primer can be used to gain chemical adhesion, although this must not be taken as an excuse for neglecting the basic surface preparation requirements already discussed. Thorough degreasing is especially important, as surface contamination will interfere with the etching process, reducing adhesion. Where possible, I would also suggest that the bare metal is lightly sanded with 120 or 180 grit abrasive paper to provide a better mechanical key for the coating scheme. Once applied, the etch primer must be overcoated with a suitable holding or protective primer.

Whatever method is used to prepare aluminium, an adequate priming scheme is essential, especially in bilges where a stray copper washer or a piece of copper wire may cause severe corrosion; indeed, an additional coat of epoxy primer is often worthwhile for peace of mind. A comprehensive cathodic protection system must also be installed to protect underwater areas in the event of localised damage.

Unfortunately, the choice of antifoulings for aluminium yachts is rather limited, as most so-called 'copper-based' antifoulings are likely to promote serious corrosion. Nevertheless, antifoulings based on cuprous thiocyanate biocides can be used quite safely, though their performance is usually poor when compared with the more powerful cuprous oxide types.

◆ GALVANISED, ZINC SPRAYED AND ALUMINIUM SPRAYED STEEL

Steel is sometimes galvanised by dipping it into molten zinc, or is sprayed with molten zinc or aluminium to provide improved resistance to corrosion. These techniques provide good protection for unpainted metals, but the treated surfaces are very difficult to paint satisfactorily.

Moreover, these treatments rather limit the choice of paint coatings that can be applied: in particular, antifoulings based on cuprous oxide biocides must not be used, as they promote corrosion of both zinc and aluminium. Corrosion salts found on zinc coated surfaces can also cause blistering of chlorinated rubber primers, which often contain a residue of hydrochloric acid.

Newly treated metals must first be degreased with a solvent or water soluble degreaser (see Cleaning and Degreasing on page 58), and then lightly disked with 24 or 36 grit sanding disks if necessary to provide a good mechanical key. An epoxy holding primer should then be applied as described for aluminium alloy. When the initial priming stage has been completed, a full conventional or high performance coating scheme should be applied, avoiding the use of chlorinated rubber primers and cuprous oxide-type antifoulings.

Previously painted galvanised or metal sprayed steel is rather more difficult to prepare, as it will be almost impossible to remove the old paintwork scheme without puncturing or damaging the thin coating of soft metal.

Chemical paint strippers can be used to remove paint from small areas, but larger areas are better prepared by Ultra High Pressure (UHP) water jetting, followed by abrasive discing to provide a good anchor profile (see page 63). Alternatively, surfaces may be prepared by careful abrasive slurry blasting (ie wet grit blasting), using a fine grade of aluminium oxide or calcium carbonate blasting media. Black mineral slag (ie JBlast®) is far too aggressive, and tends to become embedded in the soft metal surface where it can promote corrosion. Likewise, caustic (alkaline) paint strippers must not be used on aluminium sprayed steels as they will damage the surface coating.

When prepared, the bare metal should be primed with an epoxy holding primer, as described for aluminium above.

◆ TIMBER

It has often been said that good timber should never be painted: this may come as something of a surprise in a book about painting, but in fact many of the better marine hardwoods can survive quite well without painting or varnishing. There is, nevertheless, the problem of appearance, as even the best hardwoods quickly become dulled and discoloured when exposed to the marine environment. Underwater timbers must also be protected from marine borers like teredo and gribble, which can quickly cause serious damage and destruction. (see Fig 24, page 101).

Unfortunately, the fungi that cause wood rot multiply quickly in the warm, damp and dark environment created behind paint films, but they are quickly destroyed by sunlight, salt water and oxygen. In the domestic paint market this has led to the popularity of *microporous* or 'breathing' paints, which allow oxygen and water vapour to permeate through the coating scheme, whereas liquid water cannot be absorbed owing to its high surface tension.

But while microporous paints work well on softwoods used to build

Fig 15 Wood on gunwale. In practice, wood rot is most likely to occur where fresh water can gain easy entry into the timber (especially into end grain) – as in the gunwale above – but is prevented from escaping by paint or varnish coatings.

houses, they have limited value on marine hardwoods, which are quite dense, and have limited permeability to moisture. Moreover, microporous paints have comparatively low gloss levels, and would not be accepted in the traditionally high-gloss yacht market.

In practice, many of the paints used on wooden yachts are designed to limit rather than to prevent moisture ingress, so that the timber does not become too dry. Similarly, they also allow a limited degree of moisture release, though not on the same scale as microporous paints. High performance epoxy and polyurethane coating schemes are sometimes used, but these are mainly restricted to yacht interiors and to high-quality wooden dinghies owing to their lack of flexibility and impermeability to moisture.

In summary, it could be said that while timber does benefit from a well applied coating scheme, it is usually better left unpainted than painted badly. Good surface preparation and choice of coatings is therefore of utmost importance, and should be considered carefully before starting any work. It must also be added that any indication of wood rot or loose paint coatings should be investigated quickly before serious harm is done.

This inevitably leads to the question of timber preservatives, and whether they should be used to protect marine timbers. Preservatives are most beneficial on softwoods, which have poor natural resistance to rot, and will readily absorb useful quantities of the preservative solution. Marine hardwoods have good natural resistance to rot, and even if they are treated will absorb very little preservative. It could also be argued that the presence of any preservative on the surface of timber could reduce coating adhesion, and should be avoided. More significantly, though, most of the better biocides have been legislated out of timber preservatives over the last few years owing to health and environmental concerns, so it is doubtful whether current formulations can offer any worthwhile protection for good-quality marine hardwoods.

Initial preparation

Where bare wood is to be coated, a good deal of preparation work will be required before the first (priming) coat can be applied, although this does provide an excellent opportunity to apply a really good coating scheme from scratch.

Bare wood should first be sanded with 120 or 180 grit abrasive paper to smooth the surface, and to provide a good mechanical key for the coating scheme. Badly weathered (or sun bleached) timber may need very heavy sanding to remove faded layers if the woods natural colour is to be restored. Don't get too carried away with power sanders though (especially when preparing marine plywood), as it is very easy to remove more timber than required.

As soon as sanding work is completed, all wood dust should be removed with a vacuum cleaner or a damp cloth, and surfaces degreased with a solvent degreaser. The use of water on bare timber is not usually recommended as it tends to raise the grain, and can encourage natural oils to migrate to the timber surface.

Very oily timbers may require repeated degreasing to remove surface oil, although where this is the case, it might be better to opt for a wood oil treatment rather than a varnish. Less oily timbers should be primed with a suitable primer such as International's Crystal for Teak[6], or coated with a breathing varnish scheme such as Epifanes Teak and Tropical Wood Finish.

As already discussed, timber preservatives are not generally recommended for marine hardwoods as these have good natural resistance to rot, but they can be useful for protecting softwoods. Remember that sea water itself is quite a good timber preservative, and it is generally areas above the waterline and below decks that suffer most from rot owing to rainwater and condensation.

Do not apply linseed oil to the wood before painting or varnishing, as this will interfere with adhesion of the coating scheme.

If the timber is to be painted, it is usual practice to thin the initial coat of primer by 10 per cent or so to encourage adhesion, after which the primer should be applied unthinned. Alternatively, a penetrating wood primer such as Blakes Woodseal or International UCP[7] can be applied prior to other coatings.

Varnishing and varnishes

Varnishing good timber is one of the more rewarding painting tasks, although a great deal of effort is required for best results; there are no short cuts to a perfect finish, but the following advice will help you to avoid some of the more common pitfalls.

If varnishing over existing varnished surfaces, these should be carefully degreased to remove any surface contamination, particularly from waxes and polishes that may have been applied during the season. Solvent

[6] Interthane plus Clear.
[7] Interprime Wood Sealer Clear 1026 in the USA.

degreasers used with clean cotton cloths are usually most effective for this task, as detergents can be difficult to remove. External surfaces should be rinsed with fresh water to remove salt crystals, as these will cause blistering of the new varnish.

After degreasing, surfaces should be sanded thoroughly with 180 grit sanding paper until the area is uniformly dull, with no shiny patches remaining. This step is essential to ensure that the new varnish adheres well, but may be followed by sanding with finer grades to improve the cosmetic finish. Once prepared, surfaces should be given a final wipe over with a clean cloth damped with some of the varnish thinner, and dust removed with a *Tack Rag* or dust wipe immediately before varnishing (see page 131).

When you are ready to start varnishing, make sure that the varnish is warmed to room temperature (20° C/68° F) or slightly above before it is applied. Cold varnish has a consistency like treacle and, apart from poor application qualities, it may fail to dry altogether if it is applied too thickly. While thinning may appear to provide an easy solution to these problems, the cold varnish will nevertheless be prone to runs and sags, and may suffer from 'blooming'. If the varnish needs to be warmed quickly, place the tin into a bucket of warm water for half an hour before use, having first loosened the lid to release any pressure.

Varnishes are best applied during cool, still weather, when there is no wind to raise dust or dry the varnish too quickly. Avoid varnishing in hot weather or in direct sunlight, as the varnish film will set very quickly, and may be spoilt by heavy brush marks and poor gloss. If varnishing outdoors, try to finish application by midday or early afternoon, as overnight dew or frost will spoil your work, often giving it a dull, milky or frosted appearance. When varnishing in confined spaces, make sure that adequate ventilation is provided to remove the heavy solvent vapours, and to ensure an adequate supply of oxygen for the varnish to cure.

Apply the varnish using a good-quality bristle brush which has been washed with soap and warm water to remove any loose bristles. If varnishing directly onto bare wood, thin the first coat by 25 per cent or so to encourage penetration into the timber, after which subsequent coats should be applied using progressively less thinner to encourage film build and levelling. When the final coats are applied, these should only need to be thinned by 5 per cent or so to improve application properties – as would be the case if varnishing over previously varnished timberwork. Apply the varnish with long, steady brush strokes, brushing both horizontally and vertically to achieve an even film thickness, while checking for any 'misses' and 'holidays' as you go along. Each coat should finally be 'laid off' with light, horizontal brush strokes, which tend to blend more with the lines of the yacht than vertical brush strokes, and promote better flow. However, excessive brushing should be avoided as it reduces film thickness, and tends to prevent natural flow and levelling.

Once applied, the varnish should be allowed to flow out and dry in still, dust-free conditions until touch dry. Mistakes spotted on areas varnished more than about 10 minutes previously are usually best left, as defects are very difficult to remedy once the varnish has lost its 'wet edge' and has begun to set.

Always avoid the temptation to apply excessive film thicknesses, especially on horizontal areas such as decks, coachroofs and cabin soles, as many varnishes will simply not dry if they are over-applied. Likewise, overcoating too quickly will cause similar problems, so follow the manufacturer's recommendations on the number of coats and overcoating intervals, allowing a good safety margin wherever possible.

Once dried, each coat of varnish should be lightly wet sanded with fine wet or dry paper to remove small blemishes, and to improve adhesion between coats. When preparing to apply the final coat, ensure that everything is spotlessly clean, and that there is no likelihood of dust or other foreign matter spoiling your finish. If necessary, wait for a calm day, perhaps during the week when nobody is working on other yachts nearby.

The type of varnish used is obviously important, and depends largely on individual requirements. The properties of various resin types were discussed in some detail at the beginning of the book, but are recapped briefly here:

- For ease of use and quality of finish, the *standard varnishes* like International Original and Blakes Favourite still take some beating, although the *enhanced varnishes* like Epifanes Gloss, Blakes New Classic, Jotun Ravilakk, International Schooner and Stoppani Superyacht are well worth the extra cost.
- Two-pack *polyurethane varnishes* are also worthy of consideration for their superb gloss retention, abrasion resistance and freedom from yellowing in dark areas. Polyurethanes are not ideal for easily damaged areas like rubbing strakes, as they are very difficult to remove or repair once cured, but they are an excellent choice for galleys and cabins, where they could well outlast the yacht, and will certainly save a great deal of difficult maintenance work. Sadly

though, two-pack polyurethanes cannot be applied over conventional varnishes, so you may have to wait until the next strip down before trying them.

- *Epoxy varnishes* are intended for more specialist applications, but they can produce outstanding results when properly applied. It is true that epoxies are somewhat more 'technical' to apply than ordinary varnishes, but the manufacturers provide excellent information sheets to help you on your way. And don't forget that epoxies have very poor resistance to ultraviolet light, and must be overcoated with a polyurethane if they are to retain their excellent finish.
- *Wood oils and penetrating varnishes* are most useful for decks, rubbing strakes and easily damaged areas, where normal varnishes are difficult to repair. They also allow some moisture permeability, which can help to prevent the ugly black fungal staining often seen on timber.

◆ FERRO-CEMENT

Of all boatbuilding materials, ferro-cement is one of the most difficult and unpredictable to paint. The problem is that the cement itself is often undercured, with significant quantities of alkaline salts remaining in the substrate. With prolonged immersion in water, small quantities of these salts migrate to the surface where they can cause severe blistering of paint films, the blisters usually being filled with a strongly alkaline fluid with a soapy feel. This defect is known technically as *efflorescence*, and is similar in its effect to osmosis in GRP.

Efflorescence is most likely to affect newer hulls and those painted quickly after new building, while older hulls and those which have stood unpainted for several years are likely to be comparatively stable. Some owners have tried to overcome this problem by repeatedly washing the bare hull with fresh water to remove soluble salts, while others have applied dilute hydrochloric acid solutions to neutralise the alkaline substrate. It is difficult to assess just how effective these methods are, but it is important that any treatment neutralises the cement to some depth, and not just the outer surface.

The choice of paint coatings which can be used on ferro-cement is also somewhat limited, and reflects the unstable, alkaline nature of this substrate. Epoxy priming schemes as used on metal and GRP are usually the best choice, overcoated with a two-pack polyurethane finishing scheme above the waterline. Conventional primers can be used above the waterline, but must not be used below water where they are prone to damage by strong alkali. Likewise, avoid primers containing aluminium flake, which is prone to being dissolved by alkali. Chlorinated rubber paints are probably the worst choice, as they usually contain residues of hydrochloric acid, which promote blistering by reacting with the cement to produce carbon dioxide gas.

Once primed, virtually any antifouling can be applied to ferro-cement as long as it is compatible with the chosen priming scheme.

Preparation

Bare ferro-cement is unlikely to be heavily contaminated with oil or grease unless the yacht has stood in a heavily polluted environment, but, nevertheless, surfaces must be thoroughly cleaned and degreased with a water soluble degreaser before preparation, as outlined on page 58. Take special care to remove all traces of degreaser before painting.

Preparation of ferro-cement is difficult owing to the very hard, and often shiny, surface of the substrate, although abrasive discing can sometimes be used to good effect. Where possible, light abrasive grit or slurry blasting is the best option, and should be used gently to lightly etch the cement surface. Grit blasting also has the benefit of 'opening' the substrate surface, and increasing the effective surface area, which assists in the removal of soluble salts while improving adhesion of coatings. Once prepared, the surface should be high-pressure washed with fresh water at least three or four times to remove soluble material before allowing it to dry.

Application can commence at any time after preparation as long as the cement is clean and dry. Take particular care when applying initial coats to ensure that the surface is thoroughly wetted with primer. In view of the unstable nature of ferro-cement, it is a good idea to apply an additional coat or two of primer to minimise moisture transmission.

◆ STAINLESS STEEL

There are many different types of stainless steel alloy, the majority of which were never intended for use in a marine environment. Stainless steel alloys contain varying amounts of chromium, which reacts with atmospheric oxygen to form a tough skin of chromium oxide, and provides excellent protection from corrosion, but also makes painting very difficult! There is a widespread belief that stainless steels are immune to corrosion, but in fact they will corrode very rapidly if formation of this oxide layer is disrupted, as often happens when they are painted badly. In view of these problems, stainless steels are better left unpainted wherever possible unless painting is recommended by the manufacturers.

If the metal is to be painted, good mechanical preparation is essential, as etch primers do not work on stainless steel. Where possible, the metal should be dry grit blasted using aluminium oxide grit to produce a good surface profile, or, alternatively, disced with a coarse abrasive. Wire brushing and ordinary sanding methods are not suitable.

When prepared, the metal should be primed with an epoxy holding primer, or with a general purpose epoxy primer thinned to improve surface wetting. When the initial primer has been applied, it should be followed with a full epoxy anticorrosive scheme, as recommended for steel and aluminium. If an antifouling is required, the use of an antifoul suitable for aluminium will reduce the risk of corrosion.

◆ CAST IRON KEELS

Cast iron can be prepared and painted in exactly the same way as steel, but unfortunately the poor quality metal used in the manufacture of some keels is especially prone to corrosion. This is chiefly caused by the many impurities found in cast iron, but poor casting methods and the difficulty of achieving good surface preparation are also contributory factors. This all means that even the best prepared and painted keel can be expected to show rust within three or four years, while a hand-prepared keel is likely to show rust within a single season.

For best results, the keel should be dry blast cleaned using black copper slag abrasive. Heavily corroded keels may also benefit from occasional fresh water washing during this process to remove corrosion salts, although the use of corrosion inhibitors must be avoided. When prepared, the keel may be coated with a full epoxy priming scheme as recommended for steel, or with four or five coats of a keel primer. The coating scheme can then be completed with any type of antifouling.

As a second option, the keel may be prepared by abrasive discing, or by sanding with very coarse (ie 36 grit) abrasive paper. Wire brushing is not recommended, as it does not effectively remove corrosion deposits, and tends to burnish rather than roughen the surface. Likewise, the use of chemical rust converters (as used on cars) is not recommended. When prepared, the keel should be coated with four or five coats of a keel primer, followed by any type of antifouling. Epoxy coatings would not generally be recommended on a substrate prepared to this standard.

◆ LEAD KEELS

Like stainless steel and aluminium, lead forms a protective oxide layer on its outer surface, although fortunately this toxic metal is almost insoluble in water, and does not readily corrode. However, like the other two metals, the layer of lead oxide hinders coating adhesion, and must be removed before painting.

For best results, lead should be heavily sanded with very coarse (36 grit) abrasive paper, or with a stiff wire brush to remove the surface oxide layer, and to provide a good mechanical key. Gentle abrasive blast cleaning can be used, although care must be taken to avoid embedding sharp grit into the soft metal.

Whichever method of preparation is used, remember that lead is toxic, and that all steps must be taken to avoid swallowing or inhaling lead dust. It is also advised that ground sheets are laid under and around the keel to reduce the risk of soil pollution. All waste must be disposed of safely.

In the absence of an effective self-etch primer, the bare lead should be primed with an epoxy priming scheme (as recommended for aluminium), or with one of the many keel primers before the metal becomes dull, or contaminated. Apply four or five coats (200 to 250 μm) of primer, or follow the manufacturer's directions. When fully primed, lead keels may be antifouled with any type of antifouling.

◆ TANKS AND BILGES

So far we have mainly been concerned with protecting and decorating the yacht's exterior, but hidden areas inside the yacht must also be well protected. Metal yachts are especially prone to corrosion in bilges, while the interiors of timber yachts are prone to wood rot owing to rainwater and condensation. Distilled water from refrigerators and air conditioning units can be particularly damaging, and is very aggressive to paint coatings.

Painting schemes for yacht interiors are essentially similar to those for exteriors, with exactly the same requirements for surface preparation and coating application. The main difference is that profiling fillers, undercoats and finishes are not usually required. However, adequate priming schemes are most important, and must always be applied to achieve complete coverage at correct film thicknesses, while avoiding excessive application on horizontal surfaces.

Like exteriors, conventional primers must not be used to protect metals or ferro-cement in permanently wet or damp areas, as the painting scheme will almost certainly fail, although they can be used satisfactorily in the bilges of timber yachts. The bilges of metal yachts are usually protected with epoxies, which have good resistance to abrasion and spillage of fuels and oil, while providing excellent protection from corrosion.

Cosmetic finishes are not usually required in these hidden areas, except perhaps in lockers and engine compartments. Polyurethane finishes are an ideal choice here, because like epoxies, they have excellent resistance to abrasion and withstand fuels and oils well, but must only be applied over epoxy primers. Conventional finishes can work well in dry areas, but of course do not share the mechanical or chemical advantages of polyurethanes.

Unfortunately, the case for painting the bilges of glassfibre yachts is rather less convincing: epoxy coating schemes are widely advised for bilges, on the basis that the laminate could otherwise absorb moisture and suffer from osmosis. There is some logic in this argument, but it loses sight of the fact that moisture will almost certainly be permeating through the laminate from *outside*, and any attempt to prevent it from dispersing into the bilges will actually increase the risk of laminate breakdown.

Clearly, moisture ingress from the bilges can pose a threat to glassfibre laminates, but only if the bilges are continually wet. Where this is the case, painting them with a good epoxy coating scheme is a sound idea, although it would be far better to tackle the problem at source!

However, cosmetic finishes can be applied inside GRP hulls with comparative ease: two-component polyurethanes will provide the best performance here, and require only thorough degreasing and light sanding before application.

◆ WATER AND FUEL TANKS

Tanks fitted to yachts are nearly always difficult to paint owing to their small size and limited access. Where possible, purpose-made stainless steel or plastic tanks should be installed, but if other materials have been used the following advice should prove helpful:

- In general, drinking (or 'potable') water tanks must only be painted with coatings that carry potable water certificates. These are manufactured from selected raw materials that do not release harmful compounds into the water, or spoil its taste.
- Small tanks are the most difficult to prepare and paint, so are best

protected with a simple aliphatic pitch like International's JBA 016 (Water Tank Black) or Jotun's Bitumax P. Two coats should be applied by brush, having first degreased the tank, and sanded its interior surfaces as thoroughly as possible.

- Larger tanks are usually easier to prepare, with adequate access for either grit blasting or discing of internal surfaces. If the required standards of preparation can be met, a high-build epoxy water tank coating scheme will provide better performance and a longer service life. However, non-certified coatings must not be used in water tanks owing to the risk of contaminating the water supply: this applies especially to etch primers (which usually contain toxic pigments), and to most non-certified epoxies.

- If water tanks and pipework need to be sterilised, a sterilising solution such as Milton® should be used. Do not use thick bleaches or lavatory cleaners, as these are likely to damage the coating scheme, and will encourage corrosion.

- Holding tanks for waste water and foul sewage (sometimes called grey and black water tanks) must be protected with epoxy coating schemes owing to the corrosive nature of these cargoes. In most cases, epoxy water tank coatings can be utilised, although the manufacturer's advice should be sought first. Alternatively, general purpose epoxy coatings should be suitable.

- Fuel tanks are difficult to paint satisfactorily owing to the aggressive nature of motor fuels. Given the minor risk of corrosion, most small fuel tanks are usually not painted at all, while larger tanks are sometimes painted to prevent corrosion of bottom seams by water. If fuel tanks are to be painted, preparation must be especially thorough, and an epoxy tank coating scheme suitable for fuel tanks applied.

◆ APPLYING PAINT IN TANKS AND YACHT INTERIORS

Tanks and yacht interiors are painted in much the same way as external surfaces, but a number of practical and safety considerations must be borne in mind when painting these areas.

Painting in confined spaces always presents risks owing to high concentrations of solvent vapour, especially in tanks and bilges where the heavy vapours will accumulate unless forcibly ventilated. Apart from the obvious risks to health and safety, a solvent-laden atmosphere will seriously retard drying, and in extreme cases will result in failure of coating schemes.

Solvent entrapped coatings also tend to remain soft, and in the case of water tank coatings will taint the water supply. These problems can largely be overcome with good natural ventilation, but in some cases (especially in tanks), forced ventilation will be required. **In view of these risks, confined spaces must never be painted by one person working alone or in isolation.**

Paint application itself is also difficult in confined spaces, especially with respect to applying correct film thicknesses. It is very easy to apply paint far too thickly in tanks and bilges, where runs and sags are difficult to see, and paint can collect in deep pools. The combination of poor ventilation and excessive film thickness is clearly very bad news for coating performance, so special care must be taken to avoid over-application. Inadequate overcoating intervals will also cause problems, so, once again, plenty of time should be allowed between coats to ensure complete release of solvents.

◆ CLEANING AND DEGREASING

Thorough cleaning and degreasing is the most important element of good surface preparation, and must be completed before starting mechanical preparation on any substrate. While sanding or grit blasting methods may appear to remove dirt and grease, they actually force contamination into the surface rather than remove it.

Typical contaminants can include mould release waxes on gel coats, fuels and lubricants, polishes, oily exhaust deposits, tar stains, de-watering fluids (like WD-40) and industrial pollutants. In addition, new metal yachts are likely to be heavily contaminated with cutting oils and protective oil coatings. Interiors are also likely to be contaminated owing to cooking, the use of aerosol sprays and tobacco smoke deposits.

Likewise it is important that soluble contaminants like sea salt are removed before painting, as they will promote blistering of paint films (and corrosion where metals are being painted). In summary, all surfaces must be thoroughly cleaned and degreased before painting, even if they appear visually clean.

A wide variety of degreasing methods are used in general industry, but those used for yacht painting are chiefly solvent wiping and water soluble detergents. Both techniques have their merits, but in most cases it will be the size of area being prepared that determines the method used.

Solvent degreasing

Small areas can be degreased by solvent wiping with clean cloths, although great care is needed to avoid redistributing the contaminants elsewhere on the surface. A good supply of clean cotton cloths will be required for this procedure, and a degreasing solvent recommended by the paint manufacturer (as not all are suitable).

One cloth should be wetted with solvent, and the surface rubbed vigorously to soften, dissolve and remove contamination. A second cloth should then be used to wipe the surface dry *before* the solvent has evaporated. These cloths must be turned and changed frequently to avoid spreading the contamination elsewhere; how often depends on how much contamination is present, but as a guide I would suggest that a pair of fresh cloths are used for each square metre or square yard degreased. The working area must also be well ventilated during this procedure to minimise the risk of fire and inhalation of solvent vapours.

Surfaces should be degreased *at least* twice when using the 'two cloth' degreasing method.

Water soluble degreasing

Where large areas or confined spaces are being prepared, degreasing with a water soluble degreaser is usually a safer and more cost effective option; this method also provides the added benefit of dissolving water soluble contaminants such as sea salt, which may otherwise cause paint film blistering and corrosion. Instructions for using water soluble degreasers vary, but the following guidelines should be found helpful:

- Wet a clean cotton cloth or a sponge with the degreaser, and apply generously to the surface with a vigorous, circular, rubbing motion. Ensure that the entire surface is thoroughly wetted. Allow the degreaser to work for the specified period (usually 10–15 minutes), before rinsing off with copious quantities of fresh water. Continue rinsing until the wet surface no longer has a soapy feel. (*Note*: This stage is very important).
- During rinsing, the water should form a continuous film on the surface, confirming that all wax and grease has been removed, but if the water forms beads, or if the surface is found difficult to wet, the degreasing process must be repeated.
- Thorough removal of the degreaser is very important, as the presence of any water soluble material under the paint film will tend to sepa-

rate the coating scheme from the substrate, causing detachment. Some degreasers are quite persistent, and require a great deal of water washing to remove them: if in doubt, continue washing until there is no trace of soapiness, and then wash again. If available, litmus papers can be used to check for the presence of degreaser, as most are alkaline. I would also remind readers that strongly alkaline industrial degreasers must not be used on aluminium or aluminium sprayed surfaces, as they will damage the metal.

◆ SILICONE CONTAMINATION

Contamination from silicone rubber sealants and some de-watering sprays is often difficult to remove, and will cause *cissing* or 'fish eyes' (see page 128) if not eliminated before painting (see Fig 16). Some silicone polishes may cause similar defects, but will usually be easier to remove.

Polyurethane finishes and glaze coats are the most prone to cissing, but any coating may be affected. In practice, it will often be found that only the finish coats suffer, while previously applied primers and undercoats have been applied without difficulty. This situation is undoubtedly frustrating, but finishing coats are far more prone to this type of defect owing

Fig 16 Cissing caused by silicone contamination.

to their lower pigment loading and more liquid flow characteristics.

Contamination from silicone rubber sealants will most often be found near to fittings where the sealant has been used as a bedding compound, and on topsides areas where silicone rubber may have been used under rubbing strakes, etc.

Thorough solvent degreasing using plenty of clean cotton cloths is usually the most effective means of overcoming cissing, but is not always successful.

If contamination is very persistent, sanding the affected surface with some 800 or 1000 grit 'wet or dry' paper, wetted with white spirit, will usually do the trick. Silicone anti-cissing agents are available, but their use demands extreme caution, as excessive additions can often make matters worse. Moreover, any subsequent coats are even more likely to ciss, and intercoat adhesion will be reduced.

If the above treatment is unsuccessful, examine the surface closely for any minute pinholes. These are particularly common in gel coats, producing symptoms that can easily be mistaken for silicone contamination. Pinholing is discussed in greater detail on page 31.

5 | Paint removing methods

So far, we have mainly been concerned with the successful application of new paint schemes, but when these reach the end of their useful lives, an effective means of removal will be required.

Many new and improved paint strippers have been introduced over the past few years, most of which can quickly and effectively remove conventional paints and varnishes without the health and environmental risks of the old methylene chloride paint removers.

Some paint removers, such as International Paint's new Interstrip product can even be used on glassfibre hulls without risk of damage; although this does not apply to all paint removers, so read the instructions and the safety information panel before using! Similarly, if you use any type of paint stripper to remove antifouling, there's a good chance that you'll destroy, or at least damage any (non-epoxy) priming scheme beneath it, so investigate this possibility before starting work. Please also note that older paint removers which contain methylene chloride (also known as dichloromethane) must not be used on glassfibre, as they damage polyester resins.

However, even the most powerful paint strippers will be found slow or ineffective for the removal of two-component epoxies and polyurethanes, whilst there will be many other situations where the use of chemical strippers is impractical or inappropriate. Where this is the case, sanding or blast cleaning may be the only practical option.

Of these methods, abrasive blast cleaning is the fastest and most effective method, and can be used on most substrates except varnished timberwork and glassfibre above water, though clearly this is a professional operation. Alternatively, paint may be sanded off with power sanders: but this is a painfully slow process, and is difficult to use except on fairly flat surfaces. Care is also needed in the choice of equipment, as some power sanders can leave gouge marks in gel coats and soft surfaces that are difficult and time consuming to fill.

Electric hot-air guns and blowtorches are occasionally used for stripping paint from yachts, although their use is fraught with problems. These tools are very effective for removing conventional coatings from timber, and as long as the wood is not scorched, they are quite satisfactory.

However, it is dangerous to burn off epoxies, polyurethanes or any type of antifouling owing to the risk of toxic fumes. Moreover, removal of two-pack coatings requires very much higher temperatures than conventional materials, and may well result in damage to the timber. Less obviously, paints containing Teflon® must not be burnt off, as they can decompose at high temperatures to liberate dangerous hydrofluoric acid.

Whilst on this subject, heat must never be used to remove paint from glassfibre owing to the risk of fire, and the likelihood of delamination. Use on metals is also likely to be unsuccessful owing to the rapid dissipation of heat, and the poor standard of surface preparation achieved.

◆ USE OF PAINT STRIPPERS

Most paint strippers are very aggressive to the skin, so all contact must be avoided. In particular, the use of protective gloves, overalls and safety glasses is strongly recommended. Ensure that all work is carried out in very well ventilated conditions, as the solvents released from some paint strippers can be extremely dangerous in confined spaces. Do *not* use paint strippers in tanks, bilges or engine rooms, and do not allow smoking, welding, or the use of any naked flames. *Most importantly, read and understand the instructions and any safety warnings before starting work!* Effective paint removal is all about maximising exposure to active materials in the stripper, so they are usually best applied in cool, still conditions when the rate of solvent evaporation is slowest.

Paint and varnish strippers should be applied as thickly as possible with a paintbrush, and allowed to work for at least 15–20 minutes, or as directed. By this time, the paint should have started to bubble or lift noticeably, but if it has not, some further stripper should be added to replenish the supply of stripping agent. When the paint has softened or bubbled sufficiently, the paint should be scraped off with a metal scraper, and disposed of safely into a metal container like an old paint tin.

If the old paint scheme is very thick, the stripping process may need to be repeated several times, although work should become easier as the coatings start to soften. When all of the old coatings have been removed, the surface must be thoroughly degreased to remove the waxes used in paint strippers to reduce evaporation. This is usually best carried out with a solvent degreaser, although water soluble degreasers can also be used. The surface can then be thoroughly sanded with a suitable grade of sandpaper in preparation for priming.

Antifoulings are removed in much the same way as other paints, except that the antifouling paints tend to dissolve rather than bubble, and so are usually best removed with a rubber blade, or by wiping off. Once clean, the surface can be degreased and prepared for repainting in the normal way.

Coating specifications and | 6
product application

A painting scheme is comprised of a series of coatings, which together provide optimum adhesion, protection and cosmetic appearance for any given substrate. This can be thought of as a kit of parts, which is assembled together in a type of 'paint sandwich', as shown in Fig 17.

Many of these coatings provide little or no protection when used on their own, but in combination they are almost impregnable. The flow charts in Figs 18 and 19 will give a better idea of how this kit of parts is assembled, although this is not exhaustive.

To avoid confusion, a separate flow chart has been used for glassfibre (Fig 19), and is rather different from the chart for metals and timber: this is because glassfibre gel coats behave very much like a cured paint coating, and have different requirements from bare metals or timber. Moreover, glassfibre does not have to be protected in the same way as the former substrate (unless of course an osmosis prevention or treatment scheme is to be applied).

The initial primer is chosen to provide optimum adhesion to the substrate, even though it may provide little protection by itself. (Etch primers are a good example here.) Inevitably, the formulation of this primer is very much dictated by the material being painted: some primers are formulated to react chemically with the substrate, while others rely on good surface-wetting properties and a good mechanical key.

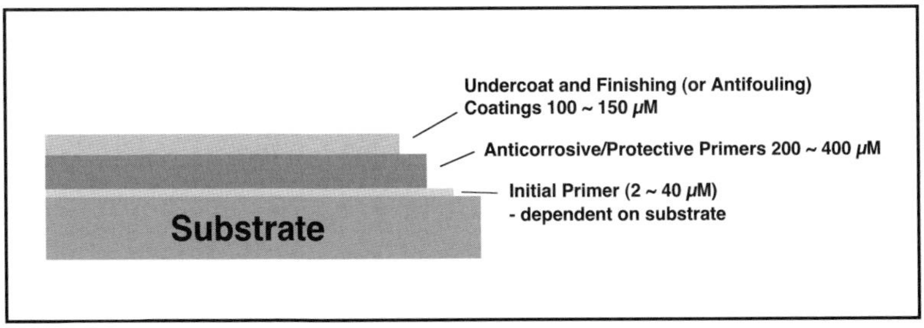

Undercoat and Finishing (or Antifouling) Coatings 100 ~ 150 μM

Anticorrosive/Protective Primers 200 ~ 400 μM

Initial Primer (2 ~ 40 μM) - dependent on substrate

Substrate

Fig 17 Step coated painting scheme.

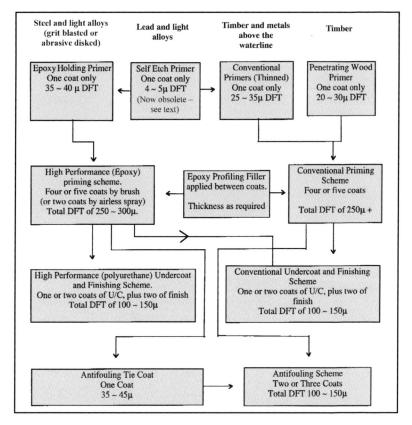

Fig 18 Flow chart showing coating schemes for metal and timber.

In many cases, standard primers can be used for initial priming, although they will usually need to be thinned by 5–10 per cent to improve wetting and penetration. Some can also be used as holding primers: to hold back corrosion on steel and alloy until a full coating scheme can be applied.

As we have already said, the initial primer provides only limited protection for the substrate, and in any case will be quite thin, so a much thicker protective or anticorrosive primer is needed to provide a barrier against moisture ingress and oxygen. The performance of many priming schemes is enhanced by the use of flake-like (lamellar) pigments; the total thickness of this protective priming scheme is nevertheless very important, and plays a large part in protecting the substrate.

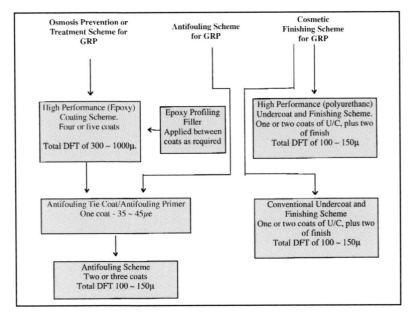

Fig 19 Flow chart showing coating schemes for GRP.

In most priming schemes, a total dry film thickness of *at least* 200 μ (7.8 mils) is required, equating to four or five coats applied by brush at 45–50 μ (1.7–2.0 mils) DFT each; alternatively, some high build epoxy primers can be airless sprayed at much higher thicknesses, allowing the use of just two or three coats at 110–150 μ (4.3–5.9 mils) DFT each.

Some coating schemes also include filling and fairing stages, where special low density epoxy fillers are used to achieve a standard of fairness at least as good as that seen on glassfibre yachts. Unfortunately, fillers can be prone to moisture absorption, and have limited adhesion to bare substrates, so by convention they are always applied *between* coats of primer. In addition, epoxy fillers have occasionally been shown to cause yellowing of light-coloured polyurethane finishes. While the exact cause of this problem is not fully understood, overcoating with an adequate priming and undercoating scheme will prevent, or at least delay, the onset of any yellowing.

The cosmetic appearance of primers is invariably poor, so when the priming stage is completed, a cosmetic finishing scheme is applied. An undercoat is usually applied first to obliterate the colour of the primer, and can easily be sanded smooth before the finishing coats are applied. Undercoats also have better adhesion to primers than gloss finishes, and so help to maintain the integrity of the completed scheme.

Where antifoulings are to be applied, an antifouling tie coat (sometimes called an antifouling primer) is usually applied to the main priming scheme first. Antifouling tie coats are formulated primarily to bond the comparatively weak antifouling coating to the main priming scheme, and must be applied and overcoated within strictly defined time limits.

We shall now look at a cross section of painting products, discussing where they would be used, and how best to apply them. While these will be introduced as generic types, a short list of examples from the main manufacturers will be included with each. Varnishes and antifoulings are not included in this section, but are discussed in greater detail on pages 49 and 96 respectively.

◆ CLEAR WOOD PRIMERS

Clear wood primers fall into two main groups. The most widely used are the moisture-cured polyurethanes, which are essentially polyurethane curing agents formulated to react with natural moisture in timber to form a hard film of urea. These include International's Universal Clear Primer[9], and Blakes Woodseal. The second group are the clear epoxies, such as those manufactured by SP Systems and Wessex Resins.

The main benefit of moisture-cured wood primers is their tolerance to poor application conditions with little risk of undercure. However, excess application must be avoided, as the curing reaction liberates tiny bubbles of carbon dioxide gas, which can give thick films a rather milky or cloudy appearance. Moisture-cured primers are usually applied as a single coat only, although additional coats can be applied if overcoating intervals are followed very carefully.

Thinned two-component polyurethane varnishes can also be applied directly to timber, although they need better application conditions than moisture-cured types, and may suffer from undercure if the moisture content of the timber is too high.

Clear epoxy wood primers are less widely used, but tend to find more specialist applications on small, high-quality wooden racing dinghies and some new wooden yachts. Epoxies have excellent adhesion to bare wood,

---

[9] Interprime Wood Sealer Clear 1026 in the USA

but must be overcoated with a two-pack polyurethane for a lasting gloss. Epoxies also need better application conditions than polyurethanes, as they tend to suffer from undercure and amine sweating in cold or damp conditions.

Use and application

Read and follow the manufacturer's safety advice before using any paint product. Further information can be found in the section entitled Health and Safety when Using Paints, starting on page 122.

Bare timber should be prepared by sanding with 120 or 180 grit paper to smooth the surface, and to provide a good mechanical key. As soon as sanding work has been completed, all wood dust should be removed with a vacuum cleaner or a damp cloth, and surfaces degreased with a solvent degreaser. (See page 49 for further details of this procedure.) Water should not be used on bare timber as it tends to raise the grain, and may encourage natural oils to migrate to the surface. Finally, any surface dust should be removed with a Tack Rag, or dust wipe immediately before priming (see page 131).

Apply the primer thinly with a good-quality bristle brush, taking care to work it well into the wood surface, and especially into exposed end grain. If using a polyurethane primer, avoid the temptation to apply excessive film thicknesses, as this may result in clouding due to bubbles of carbon dioxide within the film. This is especially important on horizontal areas such as decks and cabin soles, where it is easy to apply too much material.

Once applied, the primer should be allowed to dry in still, dust-free conditions until touch dry. When completely dry, the primer can be lightly sanded or *de-nibbed* to remove any small bits or brush hairs that may have become trapped. Any surface dust should then be removed with a Tack Rag or dust wipe shortly before further coats are applied.

Overcoating intervals for all of these products are fairly critical, and must be rigorously observed to ensure adequate intercoat adhesion; if for any reason the recommended overcoating interval is exceeded, the primer must be thoroughly sanded before overcoating. If epoxy primers are being used, these should also be closely examined for signs of amine sweating, which will be evident as a thin, sticky surface film; if there is any suspicion that amine sweat is present, the surface *must* be washed thoroughly with fresh water, and then sanded before proceeding.

Summary and typical specifications

Some examples of penetrating wood primers and their recommended application are as follows:

Clear wood primers

Product	Film thickness	No of coats	Overcoating times (Min–Max at 15°C)
Blakes Woodseal	75 µ wet–25 µ dry	One or two	8–24 hours
International Universal Clear Primer (UCP)	52 µ wet–25 µ dry	One only (see text)	12–28 hours
Perfection for Teak (for oily timbers)	55 µ wet–30 µ dry	At least four (see text)	14 hours–3 days
SP Systems Eposeal	50 µ wet–13 µ dry	One only	1–24 hours
Wessex Resin Systems WEST System 105/207 Epo	120 µ wet and dry	One or more	9–24 hours (check)

Apply to: Bare timber. Can also be used on some porous substrates

Overcoat with:
Conventional varnishes
High performance polyurethane varnishes and painting schemes
Conventional primers and undercoats (topsides only)
Epoxy varnishing schemes (apply over epoxy primers only)

Notes:
- Avoid over-application.
- Adhere closely to recommended overcoating intervals to ensure good intercoat adhesion.
- International's Perfection for Teak product is formulated for use on oily timbers, and can be used as a single-coat primer for other coating schemes.
- Epoxies must be checked for amine sweating before overcoating.
- Air-fed respirators must be worn if applying polyurethanes by spray.

Shelf life: At least five years in an unopened tin. Moisture-cured polyurethanes are prone to hardening if contaminated with moisture.

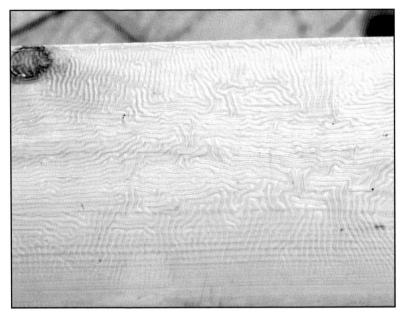

Conventional paints and varnishes are prone to wrinkle if applied at excessive thicknesses, or if overcoated too quickly.

◆ ETCH PRIMERS

Etch primers are now largely obsolete in the marine industry, as the enforced removal of chromate pigments (which are toxic) has resulted in a significant loss of performance. Accordingly, the paint manufacturers now recommend that, wherever possible, all metals should be prepared by abrasive blast cleaning, or by thorough abrasive discing with 24 or 36 grit disks, followed by direct application of an epoxy holding primer to the bare metal.

Supplies of 'chromate-free' self etch primers will probably be available for several years, but their exterior performance is likely to be poor. I would therefore recommend that, wherever possible, chromate-free etch primers should not be used on exterior surfaces, or in bilges where water is likely to collect.

If you have some old etch primer it is likely to remain in useable condition for up to five years, although chromate pigments are prone to hard settlement. If over three years old, apply to a piece of scrap aluminium, and check for colour change before use.

◆ HOLDING PRIMERS

Holding primers are used to provide temporary protection for freshly prepared metals until a full coating scheme can be applied, and to overcoat etch primers (where used).

Some holding primers (such as International's Interguard Primer Red) are purpose-made products, while others are standard epoxy primers thinned by a specified percentage. Both can work equally well.

Being the very first coating in a painting scheme, a holding primer is arguably the most important of all, as failure at this point will result in loss of the entire scheme. It is therefore essential that the primer is correctly applied and cured if the coating scheme is to be reliable. In particular, the manufacturers recommended film thicknesses must be closely observed, as some holding primers are prone to splitting if over-applied.

Use and application

Read and follow the manufacturer's safety advice before using any paint product. Further information can be found in the Health and Safety when Using Paints section, starting on page 122.

Steel must have been thoroughly degreased, and then grit blasted to Sa 2½ or Sa 3 before a holding primer is applied. Abrasive discing is also acceptable provided that the necessary standard of surface cleanliness and profile is achieved.

Aluminium must have been degreased and then grit blasted with aluminium oxide grit to achieve a surface profile of at least 50–75 μ. Discing with 24 or 36 grit abrasive is also acceptable provided that a similar surface profile is attained.

Surfaces must be clean and dry before painting, and should ideally have been vacuum cleaned to remove any blasting debris. The primer must then be applied before the metal becomes discoloured or corroded, preferably within three or four hours of preparation.

The base and curing agent components should be mixed together about half an hour before they are required, to allow a short induction period. Make sure that the contents of the base component tin are thoroughly mixed before use, as the heavy pigments are prone to settling. Furthermore, do not be tempted to add more curing agent than specified, as this can result in undercure, and will encourage amine sweating.

Commercial holding primers are usually formulated for spray application, though many can also be applied by brush or roller. If using one of the latter methods, take particular care to thoroughly wet the surface with primer, working the paint into any pits or voids. Whichever method is used, care must be taken to avoid excess application, as holding primers are prone to splitting if applied too thickly. This is especially relevant when painting horizontal surfaces and areas like bilges, where it is easy to apply far too much material. If in doubt, too little is usually better than too much. The procedure for measuring wet film thickness is explained on page 90.

Once applied, most holding primers can be overcoated up to six months later, provided that surface contamination is first removed (see Cleaning and Degreasing on page 58). Where epoxy profiling fillers are to be applied, overcoating should usually be started within a few days, although – as always – the manufacturer's recommendations should be followed closely.

Summary and typical specifications

Some examples of holding primers and their recommended applications are shown overleaf:

Holding primers

Product	Film thickness	No of coats	Overcoating times (Min–Max at 15°C)
Awlgrip Hullguard ER	100 μ wet–50 μ dry	One only	6 hours–3 months
Blakes Epoxy Primer Undercoat	125 μ wet–64 μ dry	One only	1–24 hours
International Interprime 820 Thinned 15%	125 μ wet–65 μ dry	One only	16 hours–6 months
Interprotect	110 μ wet–50 μ dry	One	5 hours–6 months

Apply to: Bare or etch primed metals
Approved shop primers

Overcoat with:
Epoxy anticorrosive primers
Epoxy profiling fillers
Conventional primers and undercoats (topsides only)

Notes:
• Avoid over-application.
• Steel must be grit blasted or abrasive disced before priming.
• Use an etch primer on alloys if a surface profile of 50–75 μ (2–3 mils) cannot be achieved.

Shelf life: At least five years in an unopened tin, although pigments may be prone to settling.

◆ PROFILING FILLERS

Profiling fillers are mostly used on metal yachts to smooth out distortions caused by welding, and to restore the underwater profile of GRP hulls after osmosis treatment. With practice, near-perfect hull fairness can be achieved, although filling on this scale is a major operation requiring large volumes of filler and a great deal of expertise; however, localised filling is quite easy to accomplish, and can be carried out using simple tools.

All of the fillers discussed here are manufactured from solvent-free epoxy resins, filled with hollow glass or polypropylene microspheres to minimise weight, and to make the filler easier to sand. Low density also permits application to a centimetre or more without the risk of sagging, and improves thermal insulation.

Epoxy profiling fillers are remarkably tough, and will withstand a surprising amount of mechanical impact provided that they are firmly anchored to the substrate. Unfortunately, fillers have comparatively poor adhesion to bare substrates, and must always be applied over a suitable priming scheme. Fillers also tend to absorb moisture, and have occasionally been shown to cause yellowing of light-coloured polyurethane finishes: overcoating with an adequate priming scheme will protect the filler, and will minimise any yellowing from this source.

Most fillers are purchased as ready-made products, although it is possible to buy individual components from specialist companies like SP Systems and West[12]. Inevitably, these fillers are more complex to prepare than a ready-made product, but they do allow consistency to be adjusted to individual requirements. (Note that car body fillers are *not* generally suitable for marine use as they are prone to moisture absorption and swelling, although they can be used for spot filling well above the waterline.)

Use and application

Read and follow the manufacturer's safety advice before using any paint product. Further information can be found in the Health and Safety when Using Paints section on page 122. Epoxy resins are known skin sensitisers, so all skin contact must be avoided.

Fillers should always be applied over a suitable priming scheme within the manufacturer's recommended overcoating time, and must not be applied to bare substrates. Where possible, fillers should be applied directly to a holding primer or an initial protective primer to minimise the risk of splitting under the weight of the filler.

Most fillers have a working life of only 15–20 minutes once mixed, so they should be prepared immediately before they are required, using only an amount that can be applied within this time. While preparation time is limited, both components must be thoroughly and completely mixed together to avoid patches of soft uncured filler.

Avoid filling and fairing in hot weather or direct sunlight, as fillers are difficult to apply in these conditions.

For large scale filling and fairing, the filler is best applied with a

---

[12] Gougeon Brothers in the USA

A team of painters using a three metre fairing baton on the superstructure of a large yacht. The filler was first applied by trowel, after which the fairing baton is used to achieve a smooth profile over several frames.

plasterer's trowel, pushing the filler firmly on to the yacht's surface and smoothing it out roughly. Once applied, the filler can be skimmed to the desired profile using a fairing baton or a length of flexible timber. Skimming will probably need to be repeated several times, with additional filler applied to any hollows. Remember that working time is very limited, so this work must be completed quickly.

Heavily pitted surfaces are best filled using the trowel alone, taking care to force the filler well into surface voids. Once the filler is applied, it can be smoothed by drawing the trowel slowly and firmly across the surface, holding the trowel at a shallow angle to the face being filled. When filling sharply curved surfaces or localised areas, the filler is best applied with a filling knife, after which it can be smoothed with a piece of flexible plastic or a postcard bent to the required shape.

In most cases, several applications will be required to achieve the required surface profile, and you should not expect to attain this in one application. But whichever method is used, excess application should be avoided, as filler is very hard work to sand off once cured!

Fillers should always be sanded before overcoating, and their surfaces checked for any sticky or greasy deposits that could indicate amine sweating; if sweating is suspected, the filler must be thoroughly washed with clean, fresh water and sanded again before continuing. If an ultra-smooth finish is required, fine finishing fillers and spray fillers are available to complete the profiling stage, although these are rarely used except on large luxury yachts.

Summary and typical specifications

Some examples of profiling fillers and their recommended applications are as follows:

Profiling fillers

Product	Film thickness	Overcoating times (Min–Max at 15°C)
Awlgrip Awl–Fair LW low density filler	2 cm maximum	36 hours–indefinite*
Ultra Build spray filler	400–500 μ per coat	
Blakes Hempel epoxy filler	1 cm maximum	24 hours–3 days*
International Interfill 400 fast drying epoxy filler	1 cm maximum	6 hours–indefinite*
Interfill 830/832 low density filler	2 cm maximum	36 hours–indefinite*
Interfill 833 fine finishing filler	2 mm maximum	36 hours–indefinite*
Jotun Lightweight filler	2–3 cm maximum	36 hours–indefinite*
Epoxy filler	3 mm maximum	36 hours–indefinite*

* Note: Fillers must always be sanded and checked for amine sweating before overcoating.

Apply to: Most epoxy primers. Check with the manufacturer before applying over other manufacturers primers. Do not apply to any bare substrate.

Overcoat with:
> Further epoxy profiling or finishing fillers
> Epoxy anticorrosive primers
> Conventional primers and undercoats (topsides only)

Notes:
- Always sand fillers before overcoating, and check for any symptoms of amine sweating.
- Fillers must always be applied between coats of primer to ensure good adhesion, and to protect the filler from moisture absorption.
- Epoxy fillers can sometimes cause yellowing of light-coloured polyurethane finishes applied over them. This can be minimised by applying an adequate thickness of primer and undercoat over the filler.
- Mix only sufficient filler for 15–20 minutes' work.
- Do not apply fillers in direct sunlight.

Shelf life: Best used within two or three years. The raw materials used in fillers are prone to separate if stored at high temperatures.

◆ PRIMERS (GENERAL)

The primers that we have discussed so far are formulated to achieve maximum adhesion to specific substrates, but would provide only limited protection if used alone. While these initial primers are important, a much thicker priming scheme with good moisture and oxygen barrier properties is needed for longer-term protection. These are sometimes called anticorrosive or protective primers, and may contain aluminium or mica flake pigments to enhance their barrier properties. Like other coatings, these primers can be separated into generic types according to their resin system.

Epoxy primers provide the best performance, and can be used to protect most substrates both above and below the waterline. They are particularly effective for protecting underwater metals (where conventional primers cannot be used), and can be expected to last significantly longer than other priming schemes. They also have good resistance to oils and fuels, and in many cases can be used inside engine rooms and fuel tanks. Epoxies do, however, require comparatively warm, dry conditions to cure satisfactorily, and will only perform well if applied to well prepared substrates.

Chlorinated rubber and vinyl primers are mainly used to protect underwater metals, and are more tolerant of poor surface preparation and application conditions than epoxies. These characteristics are useful when painting difficult substrates like cast iron keels, or where weather conditions prevent the use of high performance primers. Unfortunately, these primers are re-soluble in their own solvents, and have poor resistance to spillage of oils and fuels. They are also thermoplastic (ie they soften and melt when heated), which can sometimes cause problems above the waterline, especially when overcoated with dark-coloured finishes.

Primers containing coal tar are sometimes encountered, although their use is now declining. These provide excellent anticorrosive protection, but they also tend to bleed into light-coloured coatings applied over them. In view of these problems, coal tar primers are generally limited to use below the waterline and in ballast tanks.

The third group, conventional primers, are mostly used to protect timber, where they can be utilised both above and below the waterline. They may also be applied to bare and etch primed metals *above* water, and to timber-penetrating primers. It is also worth noting that some, like International's Metallic Pink Primer[13] and Jotun's Vinyl Primer, can be

---

[13] Metallic Paint Primer is only available in the UK.

specified as an antifouling barrier coat when overcoating unknown or incompatible antifoulings. Unfortunately, conventional primers must not be used to protect metals below the waterline, as they are prone to breakdown by alkali corrosion products.

Another important aspect of priming schemes is their overcoating compatibility: epoxies can be overcoated with almost any type of coating, while chlorinated rubber, vinyl and conventional primers can only be overcoated with like systems.

Use and application

Read and follow the manufacturer's safety advice before using any paint product. Further information can be found in the Health and Safety when Using Paints section, starting on page 122. Epoxy resins are known skin sensitisers, so all skin contact must be avoided.

If the primer is to be applied to an existing etch, wood or holding primer, ensure that the surface is clean and dry, and that the recommended overcoating interval has not been exceeded. If the primer is to be applied directly to a bare substrate, the surface must have been prepared as outlined in the relevant section.

Primers can usually be applied by brush, roller or spray, but whichever method is used, care must be taken to apply correct film thicknesses, and to ensure complete coverage. (Some primers are available in two colours, so that alternate shades can be used for each coat.) Remember that inadequate thickness reduces protection, while excessive thickness is likely to result in solvent entrapment, undercure and cohesive failure (splitting). If in doubt, apply additional thin coats rather than fewer thick coats. (The procedure for measuring wet film thickness is explained on page 90.)

Depending on the method of application, three to five coats of primer will usually be required to achieve the total recommended film thickness. As always, the first coat is the most important, and must thoroughly wet the surface. Subsequent coats are easier to apply, but nevertheless must be applied at the correct film thickness, using alternate colours where these are available.

When painting metal yachts, the first coat of primer is usually followed by a *stripe coat*: this is an additional coat of primer, applied expressly to welds, sharp edges and obscured surfaces by brush to ensure complete coverage.

Where epoxy profiling fillers are to be used, these are best applied directly to the first coat of anticorrosive primer, or to the holding primer if one is used. This minimises the risk of the primer splitting under the weight of filler, and also ensures that plenty of primer is applied over the filler to protect it from moisture and damage.

Most anticorrosive primers can be overcoated up to several months after they are applied – although, as with other coatings, they must be thoroughly sanded if the recommended interval is exceeded, and may also need to be degreased to remove contamination. However, the overcoating interval when applying antifoulings is usually much shorter than for other coatings, and must be closely observed to ensure good adhesion of the antifouling scheme.

Summary and typical specifications

Some examples of primers and their recommended application are as follows:

General Primers

Product	Film thickness	No of coats	Overcoating times (Min–Max at 15°C)
Awlgrip 545 Epoxy (2 pack)	125 µ wet–60 µ dry (applied by airless spray)	At least two	12 hours–2 days
Blakes Grey Metallic Primer	75 µ wet–46 µ dry	4–5	18 hours–4 days
Epoxy Primer Undercoat	125 µ wet–75 µ dry	4–5	8–24 hours
International Metallic Pink Primer	82 µ wet–46 µ dry	4–5	24 hours–1 month
Yacht Primer	75 µ wet–35 µ dry	4–5	18 hours–4 days
Metallic Primocon 3	120 µ wet–40 µ dry	4–5	3 hours–1 month
Interprotect	110 µ wet–50 µ dry	4–5	5 hours–6 months

Apply to:

Conventional primers Bare timber, or timber treated with a clear penetrating primer above or below water. (Follow manufacturer's coating specifications.) Bare or etch-primed metals above water only.

Metal primers Bare or etch-primed metals above and below water (see text).

High performance (epoxy) primers Suitably prepared substrates, including fibreglass, timber, bare and etch primed metals above and below water.

Overcoat with:

Epoxy profiling fillers (see text)

Further coats of compatible primer to achieve a total dry film thickness of 200 μ or more. The use of alternating colours is recommended where possible

Conventional undercoats and finishes (above water only)

Antifouling below water (overcoating times are usually critical)

Notes:

- Avoid over-application of all primers.
- Both steel and aluminium must be grit blasted or abrasive disked before priming.
- International's Metallic Pink Primer and Jotun's Vinyl Primer can be used as an antifouling barrier coat where the history of existing antifoulings is unknown.

Shelf life: Five years or more in an unopened tin, although the pigments are prone to settling. Check drying of conventional primers by brushing out on a piece of glass or tinplate if over two years old.

◆ UNDERCOATS

Undercoats are used to complete the priming scheme, and to provide a smooth, easily sanded surface ready for application of cosmetic finishes. They are usually less well bound than finishes, and are typically pigmented with extenders like talc and barytes to improve their opacity and sanding properties. Consequently, undercoats are not usually suitable for use below the waterline.

High performance (two-component epoxy and polyurethane) undercoats have the best durability, and should be applied over high performance priming schemes, or to thoroughly prepared gel coats. They must not be applied to conventional priming schemes, although polyurethane types can sometimes be applied to aged enamels. (This is explained on page 26.) High performance undercoats have good resistance to water immersion, fuels and chemicals, but, nevertheless, the manufacturer's advice should be sought concerning any long-term exposure.

Conventional undercoats are less durable than high performance types, although they are usually easier to apply. Conventional undercoats may be applied directly to both conventional and high performance priming schemes, as well as polyester gel coats, although the latter substrates must be thoroughly degreased and sanded to ensure good adhesion. Moreover, conventional undercoats are unsuitable for permanent water immersion, and usually have poor long-term resistance to fuels and lubricants.

Use and application

Read and follow the manufacturer's safety advice before using any paint product. Further information can be found in the Health and Safety when Using Paint section, starting on page 122. An air-fed respirator must be worn if spraying two-component polyurethanes.

The contents of each tin should be thoroughly stirred before use, making sure that any settled pigment has been lifted and mixed into the paint. Two-component undercoats should be mixed together about half an hour before they are required, to allow a short induction period. Do not add more curing agent than specified, as this is likely to reduce performance, and could make sanding difficult.

For best results, the paint temperature should be 20° C (68° F) or slightly above before it is applied. If necessary, warm the paint by standing the tin in some warm water (with the lid loosened) for 10 minutes or so before use. If required, a small amount of thinner can be added to improve application consistency, but should not be added to cold paints.

The film thickness of undercoats is much less important than that of primers, whose main purpose is to protect the substrate. When applying undercoats, we should be more concerned with achieving a smooth finish, with as few runs, sags and brush marks as possible. It is also a good opportunity to practise application technique in readiness for applying the finishing coats.

Like finishes, undercoats should be applied during cool still weather, when there is no wind to raise dust or dry the paint too quickly. Avoid painting in hot weather or in direct sunlight, as the paint will set very quickly, and may be spoilt by heavy brush marks and poor flow. This is particularly important when applying high performance undercoats which tend to have much shorter wet edge times than conventional materials. If you are painting outdoors, try to finish application by midday or early afternoon, as overnight dew or frost may spoil your work, giving it a dull, milky or frosted appearance.

Undercoats are usually best applied with a good-quality bristle brush, which should have been prepared beforehand to avoid spoiling the finish with dust and loose bristles (see page 114). Apply the paint with long, steady brush strokes, brushing both horizontally and vertically to achieve an even film thickness, while checking for any misses and holidays as you go along. Each coat should finally be laid off with light, horizontal brush strokes, as these tend to blend with the natural lines of the yacht. Excessive brushing should be avoided as it reduces film thickness, and tends to prevent natural flow.

Once applied, the undercoat should be allowed to flow out and dry in still, dust-free conditions until it is touch dry. Mistakes spotted on areas painted more than about 5 or 10 minutes previously are usually best left, as defects are very difficult to remedy after the paint has lost it's wet edge and has begun to set.

Avoid the temptation to apply the paint too thickly, particularly on horizontal areas such as decks, coachroofs and cabin soles, as the undercoat may not dry properly and could suffer from solvent entrapment. Overcoating too quickly will cause similar problems, so follow the manufacturer's recommendations on the number of coats and overcoating intervals, allowing a good safety margin where possible.

Two or three coats of undercoat will usually be required, and each should be lightly sanded with a fine abrasive paper before overcoating to remove any small blemishes, and to improve intercoat adhesion. Minor filling can also be carried out between coats of undercoat, using a fine epoxy filler.

When the final undercoat has been applied, it should be sanded smooth with 400 grit wet or dry paper (used wet), in preparation for the final finishing coats. This is quite hard work, but time spent here will be well rewarded by improvements to the final finish, and will be considerably easier than trying to rectify defects when the finishing coats have been applied.

Summary and typical specifications

Some examples of currently available undercoats and their recommended application are shown below:

Undercoats

Product	Film thickness	No of coats	Overcoating times (Min–max at 15°C)
Awlgrip 545 Epoxy (2 pack)	125 μ wet–60 μ dry	At least two	12 hours–2 days
Blakes Primer Undercoat (Conv)	80 μ wet–40 μ dry	At least two	16 hours–7 days
Epoxy Primer Undercoat (2 Pack)	120 μ wet–65 μ dry	At least two	8–24 hours
International Pre-Kote (Conv)	75 μ wet–35 μ dry	At least two	24 hours–3 days
Perfection Undercoat (2 Pack)	75 μ wet–38 μ dry	As required	16 hours–3 days

Apply to:

Conventional Undercoats Conventional or high performance priming schemes, and well prepared gel coats.

Two-pack undercoats High performance priming schemes and well prepared gel coats.

Overcoat with:

Conventional undercoats Conventional undercoats or finishes only.

Two pack undercoats Conventional or two-pack (high performance) undercoats or finishes. Two-pack undercoats must be well sanded if overcoating with conventional coatings.

Notes:
- Avoid over-application.
- Conventional undercoats have limited resistance to spillage of fuels, oils and spirits.
- Do not apply conventional undercoats to underwater or permanently wet areas. Seek the manufacturer's advice concerning long-term immersion of high performance undercoats.

Shelf life: Four to five years in an unopened tin. Skinning may occur if the lid is not replaced tightly. If conventional undercoats are more than two years old, check for satisfactory drying by brushing out on a piece of glass or tinplate before use.

◆ YACHT FINISHES

Conventional finishes (yacht enamels)

Conventional yacht enamels are used to complete cosmetic finishing schemes where conventional primers and undercoats have been applied. They can also be used to re-finish polyester gel coats that have become faded and dull, but will not provide the same degree of abrasion resistance as a two-component polyurethane finish or the original gel coat. Conventional finishes can also be applied over high performance (epoxy or polyurethane) coating schemes, although very thorough preparation is necessary to ensure good adhesion.

Yacht enamels should not be applied to any area that will be permanently damp or wet, as they are likely to suffer from softening and breakdown. Like all conventional materials, yacht enamels also have quite poor resistance to spillage of fuels, oils and spirits.

However, while conventional finishes do not offer the same durability as two-pack polyurethanes, they are generally easier to apply, less critical of application conditions, and less expensive.

Two-component polyurethane finishes

Two-component polyurethanes are used to provide a cosmetic finish where high performance (two-component) primers and undercoats have been applied, and can also be used to re-finish polyester gel coats that have become faded and dull.

The main advantage of polyurethane finishes is their excellent gloss and gloss retention, which can be expected to last at least twice as long as conventional materials, although they are more expensive, and may be found difficult to apply owing to their comparatively short wet edge times.

They also have excellent resistance to abrasion and mechanical damage, with good colour retention and freedom from discolouration in dark areas and on heated surfaces. However, please remember that paint coatings are comparatively thin, and are more prone to damage than gel coats.

Polyurethanes can be applied directly to undamaged gel coats provided the colour of the paint is similar to that of the gel coat, although an undercoat would usually be recommended for major changes of colour. Polyurethanes have good resistance to fuels, oils and spirits, and many are suitable for permanent water immersion; however, the manufacturer's advice should always be sought concerning any long-term exposure.

Best results are usually achieved by spray application; however, all two-component polyurethanes contain isocyanates, so the use of air-fed respiratory equipment is essential if applying by spray.

Use and application

Read and follow the manufacturer's safety advice before using any paint product. Further information can be found in the Health and Safety when Using Paint section, starting on page 122.

The contents of each tin should be thoroughly stirred before use, making sure that any settlement has been lifted and mixed into the paint. Where several tins of paint are being used to finish a large area, these are best mixed together in a clean container to avoid slight colour variations.

In the case of two-pack polyurethanes, the two components should be mixed together about half an hour before they are required to allow a short induction period. Do not add more curing agent than specified, as this may reduce gloss retention, and could make the coating brittle. Avoid contaminating polyurethanes with moisture at all costs.

For best results, the paint temperature should be 20° C (68° F) or slightly above before it is applied. If necessary, warm the paint by standing the tin in some warm water with the lid loosened for 10 minutes or so before use. If required, small amounts of thinners can be added to improve application consistency, but should not be added to cold paints.

All finishes should be applied during cool, still weather, when there is no wind to raise dust or dry the paint too quickly. Avoid painting in hot weather or in direct sunlight, as the paint will set very quickly, and may be spoilt by heavy brush marks and poor gloss.

Yacht enamels are best applied using a good-quality bristle brush that has been prepared beforehand to avoid spoiling the finish with dust and loose bristles (see page 114). Apply the enamel with long, steady brush strokes, brushing both horizontally and vertically to achieve an even film thickness, while checking for any misses and holidays as you go along. Each coat should finally be laid off with light, horizontal brush strokes, as these tend to blend well with the natural lines of the yacht. Excessive brushing should be avoided as it reduces film thickness, and tends to prevent natural flow.

Polyurethane finishes are applied in much the same way, although their wet edge times will be shorter, so application and brushing out has to be completed rather more quickly.

If you are painting outdoors, try to finish application by midday or early afternoon, as overnight dew or frost will spoil your work, giving it a dull, milky or frosted appearance.

Once applied, the paint should be allowed to flow out and dry in still, dust-free conditions until it is touch dry. Mistakes spotted on areas painted more than about 10 minutes previously are usually best left, as defects are very difficult to remedy after the paint has lost its wet edge and has begun to set.

Avoid the temptation to apply the paint too thickly, especially on horizontal areas like decks, coachroofs and cabin soles, as the paint may not dry properly, and may remain permanently soft. Overcoating too quickly will cause similar problems, so follow the manufacturer's recommendations on the number of coats and overcoating intervals, allowing a good safety margin where possible.

It is also a good idea to sand lightly between coats with a fine abrasive paper to remove small blemishes, and to promote good intercoat adhesion. Wherever possible, avoid exceeding the maximum recommended overcoating interval, as fully cured polyurethanes are very hard work to sand. Likewise, try to avoid sags and brush marks, as these too will be very hard work to remove.

When preparing to apply the final coat, make sure that everything is spotlessly clean, and that there is no likelihood of dust or other foreign matter spoiling your finish. If necessary, wait for a calm day, perhaps during the week when nobody is working on other yachts nearby.

Most yacht finishes can also be applied with a paint roller or a paint pad, and by conventional spray. Further details of these methods can be found in the chapter entitled Application Equipment starting on page 114.

Summary and typical specifications

Examples of some of the more popular yacht finishes and their recommended applications are as follows:

Popular yacht finishes

Product	Film thickness	No of coats	Overcoating times (Min–max at 15°C)
Awlgrip			
Polyurethane	90 µ wet–40 µ dry	Two or more	18 hours – 3 days
Awlcraft 2000	90 µ wet–40 µ dry	"	18 hours – 3 days
Epifanes			
Monourethane	60 µ wet–35 µ dry	Two or more	28 hours–3 days
Nautiforte	60 µ wet–35 µ dry	"	18 hours–2 days
Polyurethane	80 µ wet–40 µ dry	"	10 hours–2 days
Blakes			
Brilliant Enamel	75 µ wet–40 µ dry	Two or more	8–24 hours
Polygloss	75 µ wet–35 µ dry	"	8–24 hours
International			
Interlux Super	85 µ wet–45 µ dry	Two or more	24 hours–3 days
Toplac	98 µ wet–40 µ dry	"	24 hours–3 days
Perfection 709/809	85 µ wet–45 µ dry	"	24 hours–3 days
Jotun			
Topone	80 µ wet–40 µ dry	Two or more	18 hours minimum
Hardtop (two pack)	75 µ wet–40 µ dry	Two or more	5 hours–36 hours
Stoppani			
Clipper Enamel	90 µ wet–40 µ dry	Two or more	24 hours–3 days
Glasstop	90 µ wet–40 µ dry	"	12–24 hours

Apply to:
> *Enamels* Conventional undercoats; well prepared gel coats.
> *Polyurethanes* Epoxy and polyurethane undercoats; well prepared gel coats.

Overcoat with:
> *Enamels* Additional coats of conventional undercoat or finish only (can sometimes be overcoated with polyurethane finishes when aged). Additional coats of polyurethane undercoat or finish.
>
> *Polyurethanes* Overcoating with conventional coatings is technically possible, but is not usually recommended owing to poor adhesion.

Notes:
- Avoid over-application.
  Enamels
- Do not apply to underwater or permanently wet areas.
- Conventional enamels have limited resistance to spillage of fuels, oils and spirits.
- Enamels tend to yellow in dark areas, and will discolour if applied to heated surfaces.
  Polyurethanes
- Air-fed respirators must be worn if applying by spray, although brush application is quite safe in well ventilated conditions.
- Avoid contaminating either component with moisture.
- Thin only with polyurethane thinners.

Shelf life:
Enamels Four to five years in an unopened tin. If more than three years old, check for satisfactory drying by brushing out on a piece of glass.
Polyurethanes Five to ten years in an unopened tin, although the curing agent is prone to moisture absorption; do not use if gelled or discoloured beyond a pale straw shade.

◆ MEASURING FILM THICKNESS

In situations where correct film thickness is important (ie when applying primers), a wet film thickness gauge (sometimes called a *comb gauge*) should be used to check the depth of paint as it is being applied. Metal gauges are best for regular use, but they are quite expensive. The cheaper plastic gauges work just as well, and can be disposed of when they become difficult to clean.

To use a wet film thickness gauge, press it vertically into the wet paint coating, as shown in Fig 20. A reasonably flat area should be selected for this test. On withdrawing the gauge, note the highest reading tooth with no paint on it, and lowest reading tooth that is coated with paint. The true wet film thickness will lie between these two readings. For accuracy, this exercise should be repeated several times, and the readings averaged.

Readings should be taken immediately after the paint has been applied

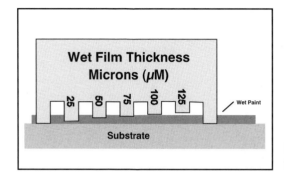

Fig 20 Using a wet film thickness gauge.

to avoid false readings caused by solvent evaporation. To maintain accuracy, always clean the gauge using a cotton cloth damped with suitable solvent between readings, and again immediately after use.

Many types of electronic instruments are available for the measurement of dry film thicknesses; however, these can only be used on metal substrates, and most are very expensive. As yet, there are no non-destructive methods for measuring dry film thickness on timber or plastics.

◆ SATIN AND MATT FINISHES

Most yacht paints and varnishes are supplied as high-gloss finishes, as these are the most popular, and have the best weathering qualities for exterior use. Nevertheless, there may be occasions where a satin or matt finish would be more appropriate, particularly for interior use.

If you need a satin or matt finish, this can be achieved by rubbing the hardened paint or varnish with fine steel wool, wetted with a good beeswax polish. This method is used by many top yacht builders, and can produce outstanding results. If a really flat finish is required, a coarse grade of steel wool should be used, while finer grades can provide a beautiful satin or lustre finish.

However, contrary to popular belief, matt finishes are just as slippery as high-gloss finishes when they are wet, and can be very dangerous. If you need a non-slip finish for a deck area or cabin sole, clear polypropylene or glass non-slip granules can be mixed into the final coat without spoiling the finish too much. These are available from most yacht paint manufacturers.

7 | Colour matching

No matter how many shades are offered in a standard colour range, there will always be those who require something different. While it is perfectly feasible to mix different shades of the same type of paint together, this type of colour matching is fraught with difficulties.

In commercial colour matching, a white or a coloured base is tinted with concentrated tinting pastes, or sometimes with another base. Both the bases and the tinting pastes are made from only one pigment, so they can produce bright, clean colours that are ideal for colour matching. Unfortunately, most ready-made paints already contain several pigments, and will often produce unexpectedly dirty shades when mixed together. (Most colour standards are chosen to allow for slight colour contamination during manufacture.)

Moreover, commercial colour matching is a highly skilled job, carried out by operatives with perfect colour vision and many years of experience. While colour computers are increasingly being used in this field, they cannot yet equal the critical eye of an experienced colour matcher.

However, if you are still determined to try your hand at colour matching, you will need a clean mixing container, a palette knife or broad bladed knife for stirring, plus a selection of different coloured paints. A good measure of patience will also help! The colours used will obviously be dictated by the shade required, but generally speaking, bright, clean and strong colours will be found most useful. Conventional enamels may also be tinted with concentrated tinting pastes sold by DIY stores, although minimal quantities should be used to maintain gloss and durability.

Start with the colour nearest to the required shade, and then *slowly* add other colours, making a note of the amounts used. Stir the paint thoroughly after each addition, and then compare the mixed colour with the required shade before making any further changes. If you add too much of any one colour, you will need to add more of the original shade, or perhaps start again.

A wet sample of the paint (ie on a palette knife) will give a rough guide to colour, but as the match becomes closer, a dried sample will be more accurate. This is most easily done by applying a few drops of paint to a piece of clean glass or tinplate, and allowing it to dry before comparing it with the colour standard.

With time and patience, it should be possible to achieve a shade something near to that required, although the colour match is likely to be *metameric* or, in other words, will only match under certain lighting conditions.

Metamerism is caused by using different types of pigment from the original colour (see page 130). While truly non-metameric colour matches are difficult to achieve, colour matching under suitable lighting conditions will significantly reduce the problem. Commercial colour matchers use special colour cabinets, but matching under a diffused north light (when in the northern hemisphere), and within an hour or two of midday during wintertime is a well accepted standard. Artificial light sources like fluorescent lamps should be avoided as they seriously distort our perception of colour, and are likely to result in shades that do not match in daylight conditions.

I would not recommend mixing different shades of antifouling as this procedure is technically illegal in many countries, and in any case, is most unlikely to produce a pleasing colour.

8 | On board and preventative maintenance

While painting and varnishing is normally thought of as an out-of-season activity, preventative maintenance during the sailing season plays an important role in the annual maintenance routine, and in the long term can save a great deal of time and money.

Any oil or grease deposits on paintwork should be removed with detergent, applied undiluted to a soft cloth, and then washed off with fresh water. Heavier or more persistent deposits may be removed by using white spirit. Tar deposits in particular should be removed as soon as possible, as they may cause permanent staining.

For overall appearance, the topsides and superstructure should be washed occasionally with a good wax shampoo to remove surface dirt. These shampoos contain additives that enhance appearance, and by dispersing water they tend to produce less water spotting than a plain detergent used alone.

Most paints and gel coats more than a year old will also benefit from being polished once or twice during the sailing season, using a good-quality yacht polish applied with a soft cotton cloth. Avoid using car polishes as these usually contain silicones, and will make future repainting difficult. If the finish has become dulled, colour and gloss can often be restored with a mild abrasive polish such as T-Cut Marine Grade Colour Restorer, which removes fragments of broken-down resin from the coating surface. Polishing will also remove a surprising amount of dirt, including ingrained dirt and stains that do not respond to washing.

Any minor rust staining can be removed with a rust remover (not a rust converter) like Jenolite® *naval jelly*. This is an acidic jelly that dissolves rust, but should not damage paints or gel coats provided that it is washed off with plenty of fresh water after use.

◆ **COSMETIC REPAIRS**

Some cosmetic damage will be inevitable during the season, and can usually be repaired by touching in with a camel hair brush. When the new paint has cured, the area can be gently polished with a cutting compound (such as T-Cut) to help blend the repaired area with surrounding paint-work. Larger areas of damage may require filling before re-painting. Where this is the case, one or more coats of primer should be applied before filling to ensure adequate protection of the substrate, and good adhesion for the repair.

Final coats can be applied by brush, but if the original was applied by spray, the repair may be found difficult to disguise.

◆ BLISTERING, CORROSION AND ROT

Minor osmotic blistering found during the season can usually be ignored: indeed, treatment of osmosis is most successful when symptoms are fairly advanced. More serious blistering usually develops gradually over several years, and does not suddenly become worse overnight. Where possible, remedial treatment should be started at the end of a sailing season when osmotic fluids within the laminate will be most dilute.

Any corrosion found during the season should be treated at the earli-est opportunity, whether in steel or alloy. Remove all blistered paintwork and corrosion products before thoroughly washing with plenty of fresh water to remove any corrosion salts. When dried, the exposed metal should be temporarily protected with two or three coats of a good yacht primer. While these patches may look unsightly, damage to the metal will be min-imised, and they will serve as a good reminder that proper repairs are required at the end of the season.

Likewise, any loose paint or patches of rot in wooden boats should be attended to quickly. Damp wood and poorly adherent paint films provide ideal breeding grounds for the bacteria that destroy timber, and it is usually best to remove unsound paintwork altogether to allow the affected area to dry, and to expose the timber to fresh air and sunlight.

When thoroughly dry, the timber should be treated with a preserva-tive, and then primed to minimise any further moisture ingress. It is also important to trace the source of moisture, as rot is always likely to occur where water can easily enter the timber, but is prevented from escaping by paint coatings.

9 | Antifoulings

Marine fouling has plagued seafarers since earliest times, slowing down ships and making them vulnerable to attack from hostile forces. The antifouling properties of copper were discovered almost by accident, when sheets of the metal used to repair damage caused by cannon shot were found to foul much more slowly than the surrounding timber. This resulted in many ships being sheathed with copper to reduce fouling, and to protect their timbers from the dreaded marine borers *Teredo navilis* and *Limnoria lignorum*, the latter being better known as gribble (see photograph on page 101).

Copper sheathing was used widely until the late nineteenth century, but it was not entirely effective, and when iron hulls and fast steamships were introduced, a more effective means of fouling control was required. This led to the development of antifouling paints, which provide a far more efficient means of releasing biocides into the water. Antifoulings have been evolving ever since, driven by a very competitive market and heavy investment by all of the paint manufacturers.

Many early antifoulings contained cocktails of lead, arsenical and mercurial compounds, although copper has always played an important part in antifouling formulation. However, strict legislation introduced in 1987 imposed severe limitations on the formulation of antifoulings, with every new biocide and antifouling formulation having to be rigorously tested and approved by government laboratories before it could be sold. The sale, transportation, storage or use of any antifouling without a valid Health and Safety Executive (HSE) or Environmental Protection Agency (EPA) registration number is now illegal, and carries severe penalties. Likewise, modification of antifoulings with additives such as antibiotics is also illegal, and in any case is unlikely to improve performance. Increasingly strict legislation and the high costs of registration have inevitably slowed the pace of development, but new biocides are constantly being sought in a search for safer, but more effective, antifoulings.

But while antifoulings are generally thought of as paint coatings, they share few of the properties that we expect of paints. They are physically weak, friable coatings, being primarily designed to release soluble biocides into the water to discourage the settlement of marine fouling organisms.

Consequently, they have very limited strength, and generally exhibit poor adhesion to plastics such as glassfibre and to other paint coatings. Furthermore, antifoulings are extremely permeable, providing no protection against corrosion, wood rot or osmosis in GRP unless used with a suitable priming scheme.

◆ THE FOULING CHALLENGE

The surface of the sea contains a mass of rudimentary animal and plant life forms, all competing for somewhere to live and grow. These organisms are collectively known as plankton, and include the larvae of billions of barnacles, mussels and other sea creatures, together with seaweed spores from all around the world.

Plankton is usually most concentrated around coasts, and in harbours and estuaries, where agricultural run-off and sewage treatment works provide a rich source of food on which these organisms can thrive. Indeed, plankton is often dense enough to be visible during the day, and can sometimes be seen to phosphoresce on really dark nights.

Everything in the sea is bathed in this soup of living matter, and is likely to become fouled very quickly unless protected by some kind of antifouling paint or other fouling deterrent.

One of the most abundant types of fouling is the common acorn barnacle, *Semibalanus balanoides*, which starts its life as a microscopic egg (see Fig 21). The young barnacle spat arrive in most areas during the spring, when they glue themselves on to surfaces with a cement secreted from appendages that protrude from between the two halves of their shells. This cement has remarkable adhesive strength, and as the young barnacles grow, they exert considerable force on surfaces to which they are attached, damaging paints and gel coats, and leaving the unfortunate boat ever more vulnerable to attack. Rather cunningly, the cement is also laced with a hormone, which quickly attracts other barnacles with any attempt to scrape them off!

Barnacle spat is carried to south- and west-facing coasts of Britain and northern Europe by the warm waters of the Atlantic Gulf Stream, although – like all oceanic currents – its source and direction varies slightly from year to year, bringing continual changes in the nature and severity of local fouling conditions.

Similar fouling patterns can be found in many other parts of the world, although it is interesting to note that fouling of this type is very

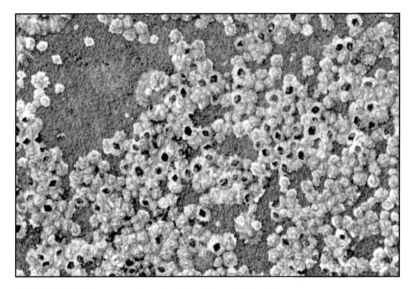

Fig 21 The familiar acorn barnacle, *Semibalanus balanoides.*

seasonal, with barnacles in particular arriving with remarkable punctuality. One result of this seasonality is that yachts launched in February or March are exposed to a strong barnacle fouling challenge, while yachts lunched later in the Spring are more likely to remain clean. Other types of shell fouling worthy of mention are the common mussel, and a group of marine worms called *Sepulidae*, which form masses of tangled white calcareous tubes, often confused with coral. However, the stalked or gooseneck barnacle, *Lepas anatifera* often seen in the days of tall ships (see Fig 22) is less evident now, probably owing to the higher speed and better antifouling protection of modern merchant vessels.

Animal fouling is not directly dependent on sunlight; indeed, strong sunlight can be injurious to many organisms in their larval form. Consequently, animal fouling is most abundant in darker areas well below the waterline, and on flat-bottomed vessels.

Anything that is not obviously 'shell' fouling is usually regarded as weed, even though not all weeds are of vegetable origin. *Enteromorpha* (or 'grass') is one of the most common examples of weed fouling, usually forming a thick green belt around the yacht's waterline, just above the boot top. Enteromorpha likes plenty of sunlight, so it is less often seen in muddy estuarial waters, or more than a few inches below the waterline.

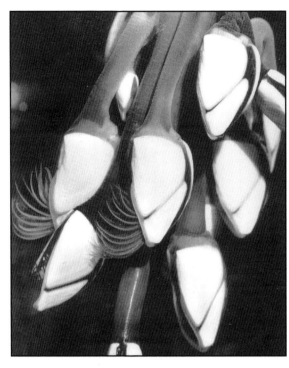

Fig 22 The gooseneck barnacle, *Lepas anatifera*.

Other common varieties of weed are *Ectocarpus* (brown) and *Polysiphonia* (red), which prefer darker habitats, and so are usually more abundant well below the waterline.

These are all true seaweeds, but there are some kinds of animal fouling that are nevertheless classified as weed. The most important of these are *hydroids*, which are related to the sea anemone, and *polyzoa*, which are related to marine worms. Both types form soft, branching growths, and are easily mistaken for seaweed, but on closer inspection the branches are seen to be covered with minute gelatinous polyps whose tentacles expand and contract to capture their prey.

Hydroids and polyzoa vary in colour from white and pink through to brown or red, but are never green. Like other types of animal fouling, the minute larvae from which they are propagated do not like sunlight, and so tend to prefer darker areas well below the waterline.

Most of these fouling organisms occur quite naturally in both American and European waters, although some are thought to have been introduced here by visiting ships. One of the most recent arrivals is the

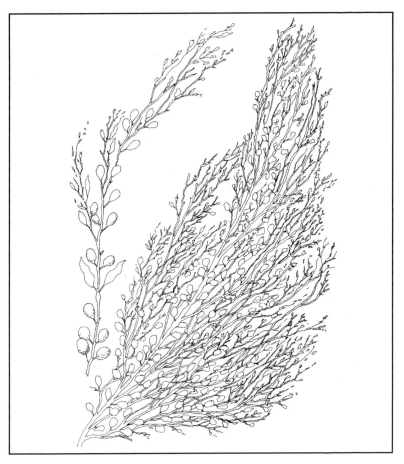

Fig 23 Japanese seaweed, *Sargassum muticum*.

Japanese seaweed, *Sargassum muticum*, which is thought to have been brought to our shores by merchant ships from the Far East. Japanese seaweed does not usually attach itself to yachts, but its large, dense growth is causing problems in many harbours and estuaries.

Another common problem is slime fouling, caused by very low order vegetable matter, which forms a tangled mass of microscopic threads. These primitive life forms are surprisingly difficult to control even with modern antifoulings – indeed, some species react with copper biocides to render them ineffective. The tangle of filaments can also become a home for other types of fouling, and frequently become so laden with silt that the antifouling is completely masked by the thick blanket of growth.

The types of fouling that we have discussed so far may look unsightly and cause unwanted drag, but they do not usually pose any serious threat to the yacht's hull. However, timber yachts must be well protected from marine borers (or shipworm), which can literally destroy a wooden hull within just a few months.

One of the best known of these is the teredo worm (*Teredo navilis*). When young, these molluscs cut tiny holes for themselves in timber, but as they begin to grow they turn at right angles to the surface, and bore easily along the grain of the wood. The burrow rarely breaks through the surface, but can extend for several metres, severely weakening the hull planking. Another common marine borer is gribble (*Limnoria lignorum*), which is a marine crustacean similar to the woodlouse, but smaller. Gribble are free-swimming creatures, which bore holes into timber about 2–3 centimetres

Fig 24 Ship's timber attacked by *Teredo navilis* and gribble (*Limnoria lignorum*).

deep, and then return to the surface to select a fresh site. With repeated boring, the timber is quickly reduced to a pulp, which is readily washed away to expose deeper layers to renewed attack (see Fig 24).

Gribble and teredo are common in most areas, but an even more destructive borer called *Martesia striata* is found in some tropical waters. *Martesia* has a large, torpedo shaped shell that covers most of its body, and usually attacks in large numbers. Rather than boring a long tunnel, *Martesia* excavates a burrow rather longer than itself, and can destroy even the best hardwood planking within six months or so.

The strongest fouling challenge can usually be expected in areas where there is an abundant supply of plankton and waterborne nutrients, but temperature and salinity also play their part. Many weed species thrive in the mixed salt and fresh water typical of river estuaries, although antifoulings do not always perform well in these conditions. Similarly, most fouling species can endure quite low temperatures, while many antifoulings stop working altogether if the water temperature drops much below 5°C (41°F).

◆ TYPES OF ANTIFOULING

With so many different types of fouling species, and pleasure craft ranging from sailing dinghies to racing powerboats, no single antifouling could provide optimum protection under all conditions. But by looking at these antifoulings as generic types, it is far easier to choose the product best suited to our needs.

First, antifoulings can be divided by biocide type: cuprous oxide is the most commonly used, and discourages the widest range of fouling species,

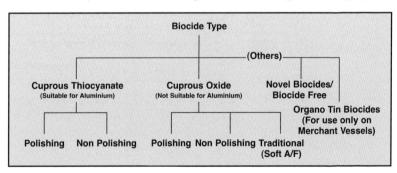

Fig 25 Flowchart showing the wide range of different types of antifouling used on marine vessels.

but it produces rather dull-coloured antifoulings, and cannot be applied to aluminium. Cuprous thiocyanate is less widely used, and is more expensive, but it allows much brighter colours, and can be safely used on adequately primed aluminium and other light alloys (see Fig 25).

The most widely used antifoulings are the controlled solubility (or self-polishing) products like Awlgrip Gold Label, Blakes Titan and International Micron CSC. In these antifoulings, the particles of biocide are bound together by a copolymer resin system, which gradually breaks down when immersed, so continually exposing a fresh layer of biocide. The paint manufacturers like to call these *self-polishing antifoulings*, while in reality the surface breaks away in small clumps or fragments, although the effect is much the same (see Fig 26).

The main benefit of controlled solubility antifoulings is their consistently good performance through the sailing season (even on infrequently used yachts), and the reduced build-up of spent antifouling on the hull. A secondary benefit is that six or eight coats can be applied for extended cruising, or simply to avoid lifting out for two or three seasons.

The copolymer resin system is simply a combination of two resins, one water soluble, and the other insoluble. By adjusting the ratio of the two, the polishing rate can be modified to produce either a 'soft polishing' antifouling, or a 'hard racing' type antifouling.

Hard racing antifoulings work on a rather different principle, sometimes known as *contact leaching* (see Fig 27). These are packed with biocide, so that each particle is in direct contact with its neighbour. As each

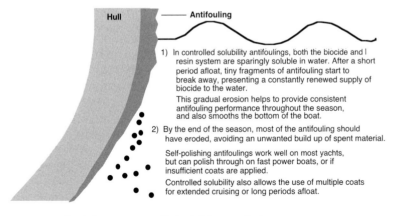

Fig 26 A self-polishing (or controlled solubility) antifouling.

particle is dissolved by water, so the particle immediately behind it is exposed, and it too begins to dissolve.

These work well on high-speed powerboats and on racing yachts where a polishing antifouling could wear through, but it will be seen that their performance can be markedly reduced towards the end of a long season. Nevertheless, hard racing antifouling is often recommended for initial protection of wooden boats when using self-polishing schemes to minimise the risk of exposing timber to worm attack. And by using different colours, it is easy to see how much antifouling has been used.

The last few years have seen tremendous changes in antifouling technology to maintain and improve performance, while trying to keep at least one step ahead of the environmental legislators. However, the next big step is expected to be a move away from conventional solvent-based antifoulings to the new water-based products like International's new Micron Optima[15] in an effort to reduce emissions of organic solvents into the atmosphere.

Some non-toxic 'fouling release' systems are now available, and are mostly based on modified silicone rubbers. These can provide good protection on vessels sailed regularly, and also offer a longer service life than traditional antifoulings. However, fouling release systems are more expensive than toxic antifoulings, and can be difficult to repair if damaged. Performance on vessels which are used infrequently can also be poor, although this depends very much on where the boat is kept.

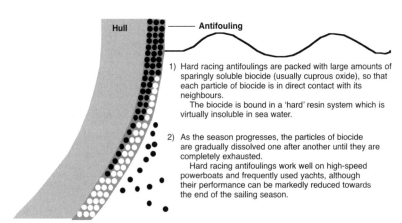

Fig 27 A hard racing (or contact leaching) antifouling.

[15] Europe only.

◆ USE AND APPLICATION OF ANTIFOULINGS

Read and follow the manufacturer's safety advice before using any paint product. Antifouling compositions are toxic, so all skin contact must be avoided, and care taken to avoid polluting the environment. Further information can be found in the Health and Safety when Using Paints section on page 122.

Antifouling paints discourage the settlement of marine growth by releasing biocides into the water, but this is very much dependent on the correct thickness having been applied. Applying insufficient coats, or thinning the paint unnecessarily is a false economy, and will result in significantly reduced antifouling performance.

Antifoulings also have poor adhesion to most substrates, and provide no protection against corrosion or moisture ingress, so a suitable priming scheme must be applied before a new boat is antifouled for the first time.

Bare gel coats are usually primed with a simple antifouling primer to promote adhesion, although, where possible, an epoxy osmosis prevention scheme is strongly advised. There are several different types of primer available, but all must be applied to gel coats that have been thoroughly degreased and sanded (see page 31 and 58).

Where an epoxy priming scheme has been applied (ie on metal boats, and those with osmosis prevention schemes), the normal practice is to apply an antifouling tie coat, or to apply the first coat of antifouling within a few hours of the final priming coat. In either case, correct overcoating intervals are most important, and must be closely observed to avoid detachment.

However, the procedure for previously antifouled boats is usually quite simple provided that the existing scheme is in sound condition: first, the old antifouling should be scrubbed with clean water, and then lightly wet-sanded with 180 grit 'wet or dry' paper to remove dirt and fouling deposits, and to provide a key for the new antifouling.

The final job is to carefully mask along the waterline and around fittings like echo sounders and speed impellers. Sacrificial anodes and radio earthing plates are best wrapped with cooking foil, as splashes of antifouling impair their efficiency, and may cause rapid erosion.

Most antifoulings are compatible with one another nowadays, but there are occasionally problems with older antifoulings and those from abroad. Where this is the case, or if the yacht's history is unknown, an antifouling barrier coat like International's Metallic Pink Primer[16] or

---

[16] Available only in the UK.

Fig 28 If your antifouling looks like this, it's probably time that it was removed!

Jotun's Vinyl Primer can be used, although it will provide no benefit if the old scheme is breaking down, as shown in Fig 28 above.

Antifoulings are usually best applied with a lambswool roller, with a 2 inch brush kept handy for awkward areas. Apply at least two full coats, making sure that the yacht's bottom is completely and evenly covered. If a self-polishing antifouling is being used, a third coat should be applied to leading edges, the rudder, and around the waterline to avoid premature wear-through caused by water turbulence.

Roller application produces a slightly stippled finish, which is quite acceptable to most owners, but for a racing finish, hard racing type antifoulings can be brush applied, and then burnished by wet sanding with 1000 grit 'wet or dry' paper a week or so afterwards. Alternatively, if you are planning to go long distance cruising, five or six coats of self-polishing antifouling may be applied to avoid lifting out for two or three seasons.

At the end of the season, the bottom should either be high-pressure washed with fresh water, or lightly scrubbed to remove spent antifouling and any fouling growth before it has dried. All that remains is to lightly wet sand the bottom with some 180 grit 'wet or dry' paper ready for next seasons antifouling. But do remember that antifoulings are toxic, and all efforts must be taken to prevent washings from polluting soil or returning to the water where they can cause environmental damage.

◆ BOOT TOPS AND WATERLINES

There are probably more queries about painting boot tops and raising or lowering waterlines than almost any other. It is only too easy to paint the water-line too high or too low, and to rectify this afterwards can be quite difficult.

If you are re-painting the bottom of a yacht or applying an osmosis prevention scheme, always keep a careful note of the position of the exist-ing waterline. This is best done by measuring the distance from the gunwale at intervals of no more than 30 centimetres (12 inches), marking the reference points with a soft pencil or felt pen.

Underwater painting schemes should always be continued to at least 8–10 centimetres (3 or 4 inches) above the waterline (or as high as cosmetically acceptable), as this area is actually at greater risk of osmosis, corrosion, mechanical damage and marine fouling than below-water areas. It is of course common practice to apply a boot top line to the splash zone in a contrasting colour, which helps to hide the protective scheme. This practice originates from the days when ordinary antifoulings had to be permanently immersed in water, so special high-strength boot-topping antifoulings (usually containing mercury) were developed to protect the intermittently wet waterline area. However, with modern antifoulings there is no technical reason to apply a boot top, although it is still a convenient and attractive way of protecting the waterline area.

If the waterline is set too low, unsightly fouling is likely to become established above the antifouling line; polyester gel coats are also likely to become stained by spillages of fuel oil in the water. Raising the waterline is usually fairly straightforward, but will depend on the substrate and any existing coatings. Bare gel coats can be primed with a suitable antifouling primer after appropriate preparation, and an antifouling applied directly. Similarly, most high performance (two-pack) coating systems applied to metals or timber can be prepared and primed with an antifouling tie coat before an antifouling is applied.

However, antifoulings must *not* be applied over any conventional enamel or undercoat, as these are not suitable for permanently wetted areas, and are also likely to be damaged by the strong solvents used in many antifouling formulations. Where conventional finishes have been applied, these should be removed from the target area, and a suitable priming scheme applied before antifouling.

Application of antifoulings over some acrylic polyurethane finishes and over thin finishing schemes applied to glassfibre can also cause difficulties, as – like conventional finishes – these schemes are not really suited to permanent water immersion. Thin films also provide limited resistance to moisture ingress, so blistering can occur following a prolonged period of wetting.

A waterline that is set too high looks unattractive, and may also make the yacht appear unstable or top heavy. Where possible, the offending area should be re-antifouled in a similar shade to the yacht's topsides, as this will make the problem much less obvious. Alternatively, the waterline itself can be lowered, although there is no easy way of doing this without completely removing the unwanted antifouling.

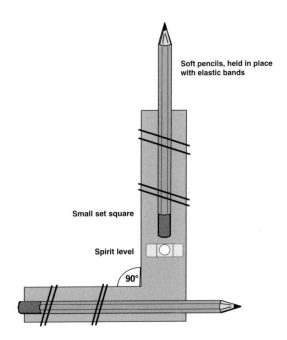

Soft pencils, held in place with elastic bands

Small set square

Spirit level

90°

Fig 29 A simple tool for setting the width of boot top lines.

The owner of this boat thought he could economise by thinning out his antifouling! The fouling itself is chiefly comprised of hydroids; an animal species related to the sea anemone.

On fibreglass boats, the gel coat can sometimes be polished to a satisfactory finish after antifouling removal, although scratching and colour staining is usually a problem; in all other cases, it is almost certain that painting will be required to restore a satisfactory finish. Unfortunately, cosmetic coatings cannot be successfully applied over antifoulings, as their biocides tend to cause discolouration and drying problems.

One of the most common difficulties when applying the boot top is achieving the correct width all around the yacht. When viewed from a distance, the boot top should *appear* to be the same width from stem to stern, although in practice it will usually be much wider at the bows and at the stern.

As long as the yacht itself is level, a simple tool like the example shown in Fig 29, can be used to set the width of the boot top correctly. By tracing the upper waterline with the tip of the vertical pencil, the horizontal pencil can then be slid in and out to mark the bottom of the boot top line, while keeping the tool level. Alternatively, if the existing waterline is too low, the vertical pencil can be used to trace a new, higher waterline. A length of clear plastic pipe filled with water may be found useful during this operation to check that the waterline is level with respect to the yacht.

10 | The importance of temperature and relative humidity

Paint dries and cures by chemical reaction, so it follows that temperature (and, in some cases, relative humidity) will have a major influence on this process.

Conventional coatings are comparatively tolerant to poor application conditions, and most can be applied satisfactorily at temperatures down to 6 or 7° C (45° F), although this would not usually be recommended by the manufacturers. Below these temperatures the drying process becomes very sluggish, with a real risk that the coating will trap solvent, and may remain in a permanently soft and wrinkled condition. Most paints are also quite viscous at low temperatures, and may be found difficult to apply. Thinning with extra solvent is not a satisfactory solution.

Low temperatures also bring an increased risk of moisture condensation, which often causes dulling or blushing of newly applied finishes. This is particularly noticeable in varnishes, where close inspection will sometimes show minute spheres of moisture trapped within the film, which eventually evaporate to leave tiny voids. Unfortunately, the only solution is re-application, but only after the surface of the affected material has been removed by heavy sanding; this is a good example of prevention being better than cure!

So how can we best avoid these problems? The first step is to check the ambient (or air) temperature with a reliable thermometer. This will give an immediate indication as to whether the temperature is adequate for the material being applied. If the temperature is adequate, the next check should be relative humidity. If the weather is obviously humid (ie because it is raining or misty), it would be wise to wait until conditions improve before painting. As a general guide, the relative humidity should be below 75 per cent when painting; any higher, and there is a real risk of moisture condensing on to surfaces, leading to detachment and other problems, as already discussed.

If you are planning to apply an epoxy or a two-pack polyurethane scheme, it is worthwhile investing in a small electronic thermo-hygrometer

Fig 30 A simple electronic thermo-hygrometer.

to monitor application conditions accurately. Instruments like the example shown in Fig 30 are inexpensive and keep a constant record of maximum and minimum temperatures and humidities. Greenhouse-type instruments should not be relied upon, as their accuracy is usually poor.

Ambient conditions are important, but substrate temperatures are even more so: whatever the temperature of the paint in the can, it will rise or fall to substrate temperature within just a few seconds of application. This is particularly true of metal substrates, whose temperatures can lag behind ambient temperatures by several days or even weeks. Apart from any problems of paint performance, cold surfaces are very prone to condensation in humid conditions. Take particular care when painting cast iron or lead keels, which can remain cold for quite a long time after a spell of cold weather. Water and fuel tanks can also cause localised cold spots, and will have a similar effect.

Where possible, substrate temperatures should be checked before painting with an infra-red thermometer, but even if one of these is not available, it is as well to be aware of the problems that can arise. If working outdoors, it is also worth remembering that horizontal surfaces such as decks can become very cold on clear nights (even during the summer), owing to radiation of heat energy into outer space, so check surface temperatures before painting.

The golden rule here is that the substrate temperature must always be at least 4°C (7°F) above the dew point temperature throughout the painting process.

◆ HEATING EQUIPMENT

In winter conditions, painting may not be possible without the help of some form of heating. Whatever type of heating is used, it must be able to provide a sustained source of clean, dry heat for 24 hours per day. (Remember that paint coatings cure for *24 hours a day*, not just during working hours!) This unfortunately rules out the use of most portable space heaters, and other direct heat sources, whether they are fuelled by diesel fuel or propane gas. Apart from the obvious safety considerations, these heaters introduce a great deal of moisture and other contamination into the workshop atmosphere, and are not conducive to good finishes or curing conditions.

Electric infra-red heaters work particularly well because they only heat the required area, and so do not have to be used in a warm or well insulated building. Unfortunately, uniform heating is often difficult to achieve, and some areas can remain too cold for satisfactory curing, while others can become too hot, especially where dark colours have been applied. Also note that infra-red heating must *not* be used when spraying owing to the risk of fire.

For permanent workshop installations, an industrial space heater can quickly and efficiently heat large volumes of air. The main drawback with these systems is their tendency to blow dust around the workshop; therefore it is recommended that the blown hot air is well filtered and diffused to help minimise this problem.

The practice of constructing a tent around a boat is a useful way of reducing heat loss, but it can lead to dangerously high concentrations of solvent vapour and other harmful materials within the enclosure unless well ventilated.

◆ PAINTING AT HIGH TEMPERATURES

So far we have mainly been concerned with low temperatures and high humidities, but hot summer conditions can also lead to problems. High temperatures significantly increase solvent evaporation rates, and the speed at which coatings cure. This has the effect of making the applied paint film set far too quickly, preventing the natural flow and levelling that usually helps to disperse brush marks and other irregularities. Brushing larger areas can also be difficult, because adjacent coats of paint will not merge together properly when joining up. Similar problems can be experienced when spray painting, resulting in 'dry spray' and 'orange peel', where the film cannot flow out to a smooth, glossy finish.

These problems are most acute in high performance polyurethane finishes, whose solvents are far more volatile than those used in conventional paints. Painting early in the morning and avoiding direct sunlight will help to reduce these difficulties, but where this is not possible, special high temperature or tropical thinners are usually available to improve high temperature application. These are formulated with high boiling point solvents, which evaporate slowly even in hot conditions, giving the film a better chance to flow before it sets.

The 'painting thermometer' in Fig 31 will serve as a guide to ideal painting conditions, but it is important to seek the manufacturer's advice on this matter, and to ensure that conditions are satisfactory *before* starting work.

Painting Thermometer

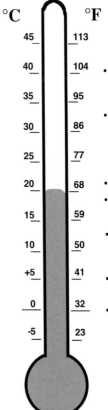

- Many paints will be found difficult to apply at temperatures much above 30°C. Tropical or High Temperature reducers should be used if applying paint by spray.

- Some paints, (particularly two-component polyurethanes) tend to 'drag' at temperatures above 25°C owing to their short wet edge times. Use a slower reducer or a retarder if one is available, and avoid working in direct sunlight.

- Paint viscosity should always be measured at 20°C.

- 15 ~ 16°C is an ideal temperature for brush application. It is also the recommended minimum for many solvent free epoxy treatments to avoid the risk of undercure and surface sweating.

- Two-component polyurethanes should not be applied at less than 12°C. Most epoxies cure very slowly at less than 10°C, and their curing mechanism can fail altogether at 4 ~ 7°C. There is also a risk of blooming and blushing owing to surface condensation.

- Most paints will have a consistency like treacle at less than 10°C, and can be very difficult to apply. For best results, warm the paint to 20°C or slightly above before use.

- 0°C/32°F - Freezing Point: only those paints specially formulated for low temperature use (such as vinyl tars and some chlorinated rubber paints) should be applied at less than 5°C.

Fig 31 A painting thermometer.

11 | Application equipment

If you are spending a lot of money on paints or varnishes, it makes good sense to use the best application equipment. There is nothing more frustrating than picking bristles out of a newly varnished surface, or trying to achieve a good finish with a brush that was probably better suited to degreasing the engine!

Of all application methods, brushing is by far the most widely used, and with practice can produce excellent results. Rollers can be used to apply primers and antifoulings where the standard of finish is not too critical, but they can rarely match the finish achieved with a good paintbrush. Spray application can provide the best finishes of all, and is very rapid, but health and safety considerations and the high cost of equipment usually limit spraying to professional use.

◆ BRUSHES

Most yacht paints are formulated for application by brush. While antifoulings and primers can often be applied with cheap or disposable brushes, all other materials should be applied with a good-quality bristle brush.

Small areas like handrails and rubbing strakes can be varnished with a 1 inch brush, but larger areas like topsides require at least a 2 or 3 inch brush. Small brushes don't hold much material, and are hard work when trying to flow the paint or varnish on to large areas.

If you have a lot of work to do, you may like to try some traditional Dutch varnishing brushes (see Fig 32). These have longer bristles than normal brushes and, being oval or round, they can hold more material. They do take some getting used to, but many experienced painters won't use anything else.

Avoid varnishing with brushes previously used for painting, as the varnish will become stained by pigment unless the brushes are exceptionally clean. Similarly, brushes used for antifouling will discolour paints and varnishes and, more importantly, residues of antifouling biocide can sometimes interfere with drying.

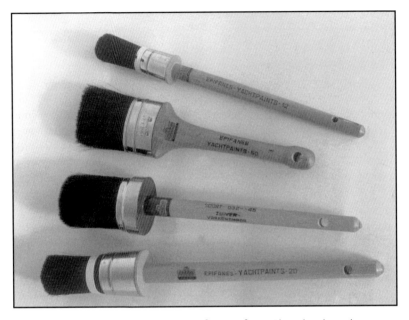

Fig 32 Traditional Dutch varnish brushes from Epifanes. These brushes take some getting used to, but many experienced painters won't use anything else.

Preparing new brushes

An experienced painter will tell you never to use new brushes for applying finishes. This is because new brushes are more likely to shed their bristles, and the blunt ends of new bristles tend to cause brush marks. However, if – like mine – your old brushes are suffering from rigor mortis in a jam jar somewhere in the garage, there are some useful short cuts:

- New brushes can be quickly broken in by vigorously brushing a piece of coarse (40–80 grit) sanding paper for 5 or 10 minutes (see Fig 33). This thins and splits the ends of the bristles, giving the brush a much softer feel, and helping to prevent brush marks.
- When this has been done, wash the bristles with plenty of warm water and a drop of washing-up liquid. Washing helps to soften the brush, and removes a surprising amount of dust and loose bristles, even from expensive brushes.
- After thoroughly rinsing out the soap, shake out any excess water, and wrap the bristles with a piece of greaseproof paper held in place with

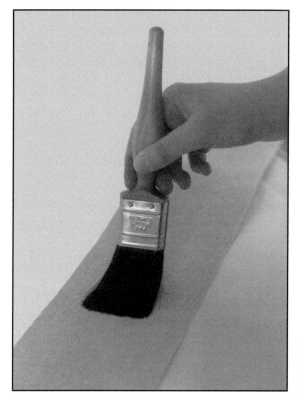

Fig 33 Breaking in a new paint brush with coarse sanding paper.

an elastic band. The brushes will take two or three days to dry in a warm place, but the results will prove well worth the effort.

- If applying epoxies or polyurethanes, brushes should either be cleaned immediately after use or thrown away. However, the cost of thinners may well outweigh the price of a new brush, so compare the prices first. Brushes used for conventional paints can often be kept fresh for a few hours (ie between applications) if wrapped tightly in a polythene bag and stored in a cool place, but they must be cleaned thoroughly when work is finished, or otherwise thrown away.

◆ ROLLERS

Paint rollers are widely used for domestic painting, where large, flat areas need to be covered, but they are cumbersome on curved surfaces, and cannot match the standard of finish applied by a good brush. Nevertheless, rollers are useful for rapid application of primers and antifoulings where high standards of finish are not required. Lambswool rollers are the most popular for this type of work as they can hold the largest amount of paint, but they produce the poorest finishes.

Mohair and short pile rollers can be used for applying gloss finishes, and will produce reasonable results, although these are more often used to apply paint quickly, so that it can be laid off carefully with a brush or paint pad. Both lambswool and mohair rollers tolerate strong solvents quite well.

Foam rollers can be used to apply enamels and water based antifoulings, but they tend to disintegrate in the strong solvents used in epoxies and polyurethanes. Special 'thin' foam rollers are available for some solvent-free epoxies, and are designed to apply these coatings at specified film thickness with minimal material loss and heat build-up. Unfortunately, these rollers have very short lives, and must be disposed of after use.

Rollers are difficult to clean, and will require a large amount of solvent if the job is to be done properly. It is usually cheaper and easier to discard rollers after use, although rollers used for antifouling can often be kept fresh overnight by wrapping them tightly in a polythene bag.

◆ PAINT PADS

These are flat or slightly curved pads, usually faced with short hairs or with a special foam. Paint pads are ideal for applying low viscosity paints like undercoats and gloss finishes, but they are not generally suitable for heavier materials like primers or antifoulings.

Pads are sometimes used to apply coatings directly from a small paint tray, but are more often used in combination with a brush or roller. This technique is useful when painting large areas, and is rapid.

The usual method is for one person to apply the paint liberally with a brush or roller, while a second person follows closely behind to lay off the finish with the paint pad. The pad must be wetted with paint before it is first used, after which it should be periodically drawn across the edge of an empty paint tray to remove any excess material.

With practice, this method can produce excellent results, and is quicker and easier than using a paintbrush by itself. The speed of this technique also helps to avoid the problems of 'joining up' experienced when brushing, although painting in hot and dry conditions can still be difficult.

◆ SPRAY GUNS

The high costs of spray equipment, and the problems of health and safety, make spray painting very much a professional operation. Moreover, spray application requires a lot of experience to achieve satisfactory results, and is far more difficult than it looks. Nevertheless, spray painting is faster than other methods, and with practice can produce outstanding results.

When paint is sprayed, it is broken up (or atomised) into billions of tiny liquid droplets, each having a diameter of only 15–30 µ. There are several different methods of achieving atomisation, all having their own particular drawbacks and benefits.

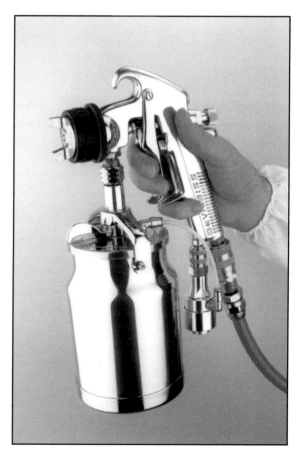

Fig 34 The DeVilbiss JGHV spray gun with pressurised cup.

Conventional spray is by far the most widely used, and works by directing small jets of highly compressed air at the stream of paint emerging from the spray gun. This type of equipment is ideal for applying low viscosity materials like undercoats and finishes, but is less suitable for heavier materials like primers and antifoulings. Unfortunately, conventional spray is very wasteful, with typically less than 40 per cent of the paint reaching the target surface; the remainder is wasted as spray mist or 'overspray'.

This inefficiency poses obvious problems in respect of health, safety and the environment, and has led to the recent development of more efficient methods. The most popular is the HVLP (or high volume low pressure) spray gun, which looks outwardly similar to a conventional spray gun, but has much larger air passages. The principle of operation is identical, but the large volumes of low pressure compressed air used in this system create far less air turbulence, allowing better efficiency.

Most other types of spray equipment use hydraulic pressure to achieve atomisation. The most widely used of these is airless spray, where the paint is pressurised to around 3000 psi (200 kg/cm2) or more by a special pump, and is forced through a small orifice in a tungsten carbide spray tip. The effect is very much like holding your thumb over the end of a garden hose pipe.

The quality of finish achievable with airless spray is usually poor, but it is very efficient, and can apply heavy materials like high build anticorrosive primers and antifoulings at rates of 4 or 5 litres per minute! Airless spray equipment can usually be hired from hire shops, and is well worthwhile for tackling larger painting projects.

12 | Fault finding

When all else fails, this fault finding guide should help you to ascertain what has gone wrong. Locate the most appropriate symptom(s), and then consider the most probable cause.

Fault finding guide

Symptom	Possible causes
Blistering (pressure within the coating scheme)	Can be caused by water soluble materials like sea salt, corrosion inhibitors (on steel), amine sweat from epoxy coatings and osmotic problems in GRP. Solvent entrapped coatings often suffer from pinhead blistering.
Bubbling	Usually caused by poor application technique, or moisture contamination in polyurethanes.
Detachment	Occurs due to poor intercoat adhesion, or poor adhesion to the subtrate. Usually caused by poor preparation, surface contamination or excessive overcoating intervals.
Loss of gloss (ultraviolet degradation)	Conventional paint and varnish finishes can start to lose their gloss within a year or two, especially in sunny climates, while two-pack polyurethanes should retain their gloss for five years or more. Epoxies can dull and chalk within a year or so if exposed outdoors.
Poor gloss (freshly applied paint)	Usually caused by overnight dew or condensation, which often causes blooming, blushing or whitening of paint and varnish films.

Slow drying	Mostly caused by poor ventilation and/or inadequate temperatures. Paint that is applied too thickly will be slow drying, and may also wrinkle. Old enamels may be slow drying because colouring pigments have absorbed the dryers over time. Check by brushing a sample of the paint on to a clean piece of glass or metal.
Soft films (solvent entrapment and/ or undercure)	Undercure and/or solvent entrapment. Can be caused by inadequate curing temperatures, poor ventilation, excessive film thickness or overcoating too quickly. Abuse of accelerators can also lead to softness. Two-component products must be correctly mixed to avoid undercure.
Splitting (poor cohesive strength)	Appears similar to detachment, but is caused by weakness of the paint film itself. (Check the back of any paint flakes for a slightly rough appearance and smell of solvent.) Usual causes are solvent entrapment and/or undercure.
Wrinkling (solvent entrapment)	Usually caused by incompatibility, excessive film thicknesses or premature overcoating.

Troubleshooting guide

Symptom	Possible causes
Bleeding	Usually associated with primers containing coal tar or bitumen. Can be reduced by using an aluminium isolating primer. Red antifoulings can also bleed into lighter coloured antifoulings applied over them owing to the solubility of toluidine red pigment in organic solvents.
Fading (loss of colour)	Usually caused by prolonged exposure to sunlight (ie ultraviolet degradation), which brings about a permanent change in the chemical structure of colouring pigments. Reds and yellows are most prone to fading, while blues and greens are comparatively stable.
Yellowing	Usually associated with conventional resin systems, which are prone to become yellow or brown with age, especially in dark areas and when heated. Can also be caused by epoxy profiling fillers which have not cured fully, or have not been overcoated with an adequate thickness of primer.

13 | Health and safety when using paints

Paint products are chemical compositions, and must be used and handled with care. This chapter explains the risks associated with commonly used materials, and gives some practical advice on how to avoid them.

◆ SOLVENTS AND THINNERS

Solvents are probably the single most hazardous constituent used in paints, posing four significant risks:

1. They are highly inflammable.
2. They are harmful by inhalation and by skin absorption.
3. They are strongly de-fatting, rapidly removing protective oils and fats from the skin. This significantly increases the risk of skin infections and dermatitis.
4. They are an environmental hazard.

The environmental hazards and safe disposal of solvents were discussed on pages 22 and 127 respectively; we shall now examine the risks to personal health and safety.

Solvents used in paints are volatile, and they start to evaporate into the atmosphere as soon as the container is opened. Once released, their heavy vapours form a potentially explosive mixture with air, posing a particular risk in tanks, bilges and other confined spaces where they tend to accumulate. These hazards are similar to those associated with petrol vapours, and with propane and butane gases.

The concentration of any solvent vapour in the atmosphere is clearly important: a certain concentration of any vapour (or gas) is required for an explosion to occur, and is known as the lower explosive limit, or LEL. (There is also an upper explosive limit, beyond which there is insufficient oxygen to permit an explosion, although this is rather academic in our case.) As solvent vapours are rarely distributed uniformly in the atmosphere, 10 per cent of the LEL is regarded as the maximum safe concentration, except under specially controlled conditions.

For each litre of paint applied, a certain volume of fresh air is required to prevent the concentration of solvent vapour from exceeding the LEL: this is known as the required air quantity (or RAQ), and should be declared on the health and safety data sheets that accompany the product.

Solvents with a low *flash point* are much more volatile than those with a high flash point, forming an explosive mixture with air far more readily. These must be handled with particular care, and depending on the volume involved, may need special storage.

The above information is important, but avoiding possible sources of ignition is even more so: smoking, welding or the use of naked flames must not be allowed when any type of paint or solvent is being used. Chlorinated solvents are especially hazardous, for although non-flammable, they can liberate dangerous decomposition products (including phosgene) when heated.

◆ OCCUPATIONAL EXPOSURE LIMITS

The above requirements are concerned solely with preventing fire and explosion, but do not provide any protection for personal health. Excessive inhalation of solvent vapours can have a number of short-term side effects, ranging from drunkenness and nausea to collapse, loss of consciousness and even death. There is also the risk of longer-term effects such as damage to internal organs. To minimise these risks, the concentration of solvent vapours in the working atmosphere must be kept below the occupational exposure limit (or OEL) at all times.

Occupational exposure limits apply to solvent vapours, dusts and other hazardous matter to which workers may be exposed, and are defined as the levels at which employees may be continuously subjected in their place of work, without detriment to health during a normal working lifetime. Occupational exposure limits (or OELs) are based on figures published by the World Health Organisation, and are continually reviewed in the light of new toxicological evidence from around the world. It is important to understand that these figures are based on *current knowledge only*, and may be raised or lowered as new data becomes available.

The ventilation required to achieve the OEL should be declared on health and safety data sheets, and is calculated in the same way as LELs discussed previously. If safe exposure levels cannot be maintained, or if there is any doubt, *suitable respiratory equipment must be worn*.

◆ SKIN CONTACT

Many people use solvents for degreasing without realising that they have a similar effect on their skin. Indeed, most paint solvents are strongly de-fatting, which means that they rapidly remove natural oils from the skin, leaving it dry and prone to infection. They also increase the risk of dermatitis from irritants such as epoxy resins. Furthermore, many solvents are absorbed through the skin into the bloodstream, where they can cause serious damage to internal organs.

These risks can be avoided by wearing protective gloves whenever handling paints or solvents, and by avoiding all other skin contact. In particular, solvents should never be used for cleaning hands or clothing, or for any other purpose not recommended by the manufacturer. The use of safety glasses or goggles is also strongly recommended.

Many solvents will cause a rash or severe irritation by prolonged skin contact, so if any clothes become soaked in paint or solvent, they must be taken off immediately and put in a safe place. Likewise, solvent-soaked rags should be safely disposed of immediately after use, and must never be carried in pockets.

If a hand cleaner is required, a number of very good products are available from yacht chandlers, paint shops and auto factors, together with barrier creams, respirators and other protective equipment.

◆ PRECAUTIONS

Antifoulings

Antifoulings prevent fouling growth by releasing toxic biocides into the water. Some of these biocides are toxic by skin absorption, and all are harmful if ingested or inhaled as spray mists.

Antifoulings should always be applied in well ventilated conditions, and a full-face air-fed respirator (complying with BS 2092) worn if applying by spray. Protective gloves and overalls should be worn during application, and a suitable barrier cream applied to the hands, forearms, and other vulnerable or exposed areas of the body. Safety spectacles or goggles should also be worn to protect the eyes from splashes.

If clothes become contaminated with antifouling, they must be taken off immediately and put in a safe place. Likewise, solvent-soaked rags should be safely disposed of immediately after use, and must never be carried in pockets. If skin irritation or a rash is experienced, painting should be discontinued until a doctor has examined these symptoms.

Antifoulings must never be burnt off or dry sanded, as *the fumes or sanding dust will be toxic*, even though the antifouling may be thought to be exhausted. Particular care should be taken to avoid the risk of fire.

When antifouling is completed, wash your face and hands, and rinse your mouth with fresh water before eating, drinking or smoking. Take care to avoid contaminating food or drinking water.

In addition to the precautions noted above, good personal hygiene routines (as recommended for epoxies) should be followed to minimise the risk of skin disorders.

◆ CONVENTIONAL PAINTS AND VARNISHES

Conventional materials are comparatively safe to handle and apply, but, nevertheless, certain basic precautions are required.

Conventional paints and varnishes contain large amounts of flammable solvent, which in extreme conditions can form a potentially explosive mixture when combined with air. They also consume atmospheric oxygen, so it is important that the area is well ventilated both for personal safety, and to ensure that the coating dries properly.

White spirit should also be handled with care as it is strongly defatting to the skin, and may cause severe irritation by prolonged exposure. If clothes become contaminated by paint or solvent, they must be taken off immediately and put in a safe place.

In addition to the basic precautions noted above, good personal hygiene routines (as recommended for epoxies) should be followed to minimise the risk of skin disorders.

◆ EPOXIES

Epoxy resins are known skin sensitisers, and may cause dermatitis and other disorders by repeated skin contact.

Dermatitis usually starts as a rash or irritation to exposed areas of skin. Solvent-free coatings and fillers pose the greatest risk as they usually contain lower molecular weight resins (which are very irritant), and, being viscous, are difficult to remove from the skin.

Failure to remove epoxies from the skin promptly, and the use of solvents or harsh detergents for washing, will significantly increase the risk of dermatitis. It should also be remembered that while the hands are *comparatively* resistant to skin irritation, the skin covering other areas of the body is far more sensitive, and if exposed to epoxy materials is likely to be severely irritated. For this reason, never touch your face, mouth or eyes when using epoxies, and wash your hands *before* visiting the toilet.

To avoid these risks, wear protective gloves and overalls during application, and apply a barrier cream to the hands, forearms and other exposed areas of the body. Safety glasses or goggles should also be worn to protect the eyes from splashes. If skin irritation or a rash is experienced, the use of epoxies should be discontinued until the symptoms have been examined by a doctor. If clothes become contaminated with epoxy, they must be taken off immediately and put in a safe place.

Epoxy fillers may also cause irritation when sanded, as some uncured material will often be present in the sanding dust. This tends to be particularly irritating to the forehead, eyes and neck, and in sweaty areas where the dust collects. Again, the use of a suitable barrier cream applied to the face, arms and neck is strongly recommended. Properly fitted overalls with elasticated cuffs are also helpful. Respiratory protection must be worn when sanding.

Good ventilation is required when applying all epoxies, *including* solvent-free coatings and fillers, as the curing agents used in these materials sometimes contain volatile low molecular weight amines, which can cause skin and respiratory irritation. Most solvent-free epoxies are now formulated to minimise this problem, but it does occasionally affect batches of some materials, and may cause problems where application is carried out in a confined space such as a 'tent' erected around a boat being treated for osmosis.

◆ ISOCYANATE CURED POLYURETHANE PAINTS AND VARNISHES

Two-pack polyurethanes offer outstanding gloss and durability, but they also pose serious health risks if applied by spray.[1]

All polyurethane curing agents contain traces of free isocyanate monomer, a highly toxic material that causes chronic respiratory disorders if inhaled in droplet form.[2] While these droplets eventually react with atmospheric moisture, they can remain active in the atmosphere for around an hour after spraying has been completed.

It should be noted that the effects of isocyanate inhalation are cumulative, with repeated exposure increasing the risk of sensitisation. Smokers, and those with respiratory disorders (including hay fever), are most at risk, and, once sensitised, even very mild exposure may result in a severe asthmatic reaction requiring urgent medical treatment.

To avoid these risks, full-face air-fed respirators *must* be worn by the sprayhand and those in the immediate vicinity whenever two-pack polyurethanes are applied with a spray gun, and for *at least two hours* after spraying has been completed.

However, it should be noted that there is generally no isocyanate risk associated with brush application of polyurethanes as long as good ventilation is provided to remove any solvent or isocyanate vapour from the atmosphere. Furthermore, there is no isocyanate risk associated with urethane modified oils or alkyds, as the isocyanate monomers are fully reacted during manufacture.

In addition to the precautions noted above, good personal hygiene routines (as recommended for epoxies) should be followed to minimise the risk of skin disorders.

◆ DISPOSING OF WASTE PAINT AND SOLVENT

When painting is completed, there will almost certainly be some waste paint and solvent to dispose of. We have a particular duty to dispose of waste paint safely, as it is toxic, and poses a fire hazard if not disposed of correctly. Waste paint and solvent should be poured into *clearly marked* drums, which can then be sent for recycling. In this process, the solvent is distilled from the waste, and is used in the manufacture of cleaners, equipment etc.

The drums should be sealed when not in use, and located outdoors in a secure area where vandals cannot set fire to them, or cause other damage. (Something like a bottled gas store is ideal.) If your boatyard does not have these facilities, you should take your waste to the nearest waste disposal site, so that it can be disposed of properly. For further advice, contact your local authority, or for large quantities contact a specialist waste disposal contractor.

Never dispose of waste paint or solvents in a dustbin, in a rubbish skip, or by tipping them into drains or on to the ground, as this poses a severe fire, explosion and pollution hazard, and may result in prosecution.

Notes

1   Conventional spray has a typical transfer efficiency of less than 40 per cent, with the remaining material liberated to the atmosphere in the form of liquid paint droplets. A well atomised droplet has a diameter of 15–25 μ (microns) and is considered to be of 'respirable size'.

2   Up to 1.0 per cent residual isocyanate monomer is present in commercially manufactured polyurethane curing agents (source: Bayer).

Glossary of painting terms

This is a brief glossary of technical terms related to paints and painting, some of which are not found outside of the industry.

Amine sweat (also called **amine blush**)   A thin, sticky film of amine carbomate which can form on the surface of epoxy coatings and fillers, usually caused by inadequate curing temperatures and/or high humidity. Amine sweat must be removed by washing with fresh water before overcoating. See pages 14, 69 and 77.

Amine adducts *see page 13.*

Barrier coat   Used to allow application of a paint which is not compatible with an existing scheme. Often specified when applying antifoulings over a scheme of unknown history, and to retard **bleeding** of tar-containing primers.

Bleeding   Staining caused by soluble pigments or binders migrating from underlying coatings. Primers containing coal tar and red antifoulings are most prone to bleeding.

Blast cleaning *see page 35.*

Cathodic protection   A method of protecting metals from corrosion in a marine environment, where an expendable **cathode** (usually a zinc alloy) is used to create a more powerful cell than the natural corrosion cell.

Chalking   Surface breakdown of a paint film caused by exposure to ultra-violet light, water and oxygen. Chalking is evident by severe dulling and powdery surface deposits.

Cissing   Small saucer-like depressions in a paint film, usually caused by contamination with silicones or other de-wetting agents. Often referred to as 'fish eyes' owing to their characteristic circular pattern.

Coverage   The area covered by a given volume of paint at its recommended film thickness. To calculate coverage, divide the volume of paint (in millilitres) by the wet film thickness applied (in microns). The answer will be given in M²/litre. Alternatively, multiply the area to be painted by the specified wet film thickness to calculate the quantity of paint required (in millilitres).

Cross linking (or **curing**)   Effect where molecules in a polymer link together by chemical reaction to produce a rigid three-dimensional structure. The degree of cure is known as the cross link density (sometimes abbreviated to XLD).

Dew point   Surface temperature below which atmospheric moisture will condense, making painting impossible. Substrates temperature must always be at least 4°C (7°F) above the dew point temperature throughout the painting and curing process.

Dry film thickness (DFT)   Thickness of a paint film after it has cured and all solvent has evaporated. Dry film thickness is usually measured in μM or microns, but may also be expressed in mil or thou. See also wet film thickness.

Efflorescence   Liberation and migration of soluble alkaline salts from cement or concrete owing to the presence of moisture. This effect is similar to osmosis in GRP, and causes blistering of paint coatings. Any blister fluid will be strongly alkaline, and can burn sensitive skin.

Film   Any single coat or layer of paint applied to a surface, rather than a 'paint scheme'.

Fire retarding paint   Generally means a paint that retards the surface spread of flame, but provides limited protection for the substrate. Often specified in areas with a high fire risk such as galleys and engine rooms. See also **intumescent** paints.

Flash point   The temperature at which a flammable liquid produces sufficient vapour to allow ignition by a small external flame or spark.

Flash rusting   Rapid surface rusting of freshly prepared steel, usually caused by rainwater, condensation or wet grit blasting.

Floating (floatation)   Separation of pigment, dyestuffs or other paint components to the surface of a paint film, often giving a 'milky' appearance. Light blue shades are particularly prone to floatation, which is worsened by excessive film thicknesses.

Gel coat   Protective outer resin layer on glass reinforced polyester laminates. Gel coats are usually coloured, but some builders use unpigmented (clear) gel coat for underwater areas.

High build coatings   Paints that can be applied at comparatively high **wet film thicknesses** (usually in excess of 100 μ).

Intumescent (paint)   Fire retarding paints which expand rapidly on exposure to heat, to such a degree that they protect the **substrate** by insulation.

Lifting Softening and disruption of a coating when overcoated. Usually caused by incompatibility or premature overcoating.

Metamerism An effect where two paints appear to have the same colour under one light source, but are noticeably different when lighting conditions change. This is a complex problem, caused by the use of different pigments to achieve the same colour. A *non-metameric* colour match will appear the same under all lighting conditions, but is difficult to achieve unless identical pigments are used in both paints.

Microns (abbreviation μ or μM) Measurement used when specifying or measuring paint film thickness. There are 1000 microns in a millimetre. To convert microns into thousandths of an inch (mil), divide the figure by 25.4.

Mud cracking Irregular cracking of a paint film with appearance similar to that of a dried-up river bed. Usually caused by application of an incompatible coating or excessive film thickness.

Osmosis (also known as **Boat pox**) Chemical breakdown within a glass-fibre laminate caused by moisture ingress, which ultimately causes blistering of the gel coat.

Overcure Condition caused by excessive addition of a curing agent to a two-component paint. Overcure causes brittleness in polyurethanes and **amine sweating** in epoxies, but does *not* accelerate drying.

Plasticisers Additives used in paints and plastics to improve flexibility. With time, and exposure to the elements, these are slowly depleted, and the films can become brittle. Soft plastics like PVC fenders contain large quantities of plasticisers, often forming a sticky surface film which must be washed off regularly to avoid attracting abrasive dirt and grit.

Polymerisation see **Cross linking**.

Pot life Period during which a two-component material can be satisfactorily applied after mixing.

Relative humidity (RH) Measure of the amount of moisture present in the atmosphere, relative to temperature. Warm air takes up comparatively large quantities of moisture, whereas cold air absorbs very little. When air is saturated with moisture (ie 100 per cent RH), mist or fog occurs, with moisture condensing on any surface at or below ambient temperature.

Sensitiser Material that causes an allergic reaction by repeated contact or exposure, such as epoxy and polyurethane curing agents. Also known as 'allergens'.

Solvent entrapment   If solvents do not evaporate before a paint film cures, they can become trapped within the coating scheme. Usually caused by excessive film thickness, premature overcoating or abuse of accelerators, solvent entrapment causes soft paint films, poor gloss and **splitting**.

Solvent shock   Precipitation, gelling or flocculation caused by adding an incompatible solvent (or diluent), or a solvent that is too cold. Adding solvent too quickly can also cause this problem, particularly in epoxies and polyurethanes.

Splitting   Defect where a paint coating fails owing to poor cohesive (internal) strength, rather than poor adhesion. Usually caused by **solvent entrapment** and/or **undercure**. Also known as cohesive failure.

Tack rag   A special cloth impregnated with linseed oil, which is used to remove traces of dust from surfaces immediately before painting. Also known as 'dust wipes' and 'tak rags'.

Undercure   Condition where a paint coating fails to cure properly, either due to incorrect mixing, or application in cold/or damp conditions. Undercured finishes often remain permanently soft with a poor gloss.

Viscosity   Measure of how thick a liquid is and how well it flows. Usually measured in time taken for paint to flow through a viscosity cup, such as a Zahn, DIN or BS Cup.

Volume solids   The percentage (thickness) of paint that remains after all solvent has evaporated.

Wet edge time   Period during which adjacent coats of paint are sufficiently fluid to merge or fuse together without leaving brush marks (ie before the film has 'closed'). High temperatures, direct sunlight and strong wind significantly reduce wet edge time, and make large areas difficult to paint.

Wet film thickness (WFT)   Thickness of a paint when first applied, usually expressed in **microns** (μM) or mil.

Wet Rot   Decay of timber by fungi that thrive in moist wood and poorly ventilated areas. Often found behind poorly adherent paint films, or where rainwater has been able to enter the wood (especially into end grain), but has not been able to evaporate.

Zinc spraying   Similar to galvanising, molten zinc is sprayed on to prepared steel using a special heated spray gun. Zinc-sprayed surfaces are difficult to paint satisfactorily, and limit the choice of antifouling used.

Conversion tables

These conversion tables are included to help when converting from imperial to metric measures (and vice versa), and when converting American measures. Information is also given for calculating the underwater and topsides area of yachts to help calculate the correct quantity of paint to purchase.

Length	Equivalent	Capacity and volume	Equivalent
1 thou of 1 mil =	25.4 microns or µM	1 litre =	1000 millilitres/ cubic centimetres 1.75975 imperial pints 35.2 imperial fluid ounces 2.11 US pints 33.813 US fluid ounces
1 inch =	25.4 millimetres 25 400 microns or µM		
1 yard =	914.4 millimetres		
1 millimetre =	1000 microns or µM	1 imperial pint =	568 millilitres/ cubic centimetres 20 fluid ounces
1 metre =	1000 millimetres/ 100 centimetres 39.37 inches 1.09361 yards	1 imperial fluid ounce =	28.4 millilitres

Area	Equivalent		
		1 US pint =	473.176 millilitres 16 US fluid ounces
1 square metre =	1.19599 square yards		
1 square inch =	645.16 square millimetres 6.4516 square centimetres	1 US fluid ounce =	29.574 millilitres
		1 imperial gallon =	4.54609 litres
		1 US gallon =	3.78541 litres

Weight	Equivalent	Pressure	Equivalent
1 kilogram =	1000 grams	1 bar	14.5038 lbf/in² (psi)
	2.20462 pounds	1 std	14.6959 lbf/in² (psi)
1 pound =	453.59237 grams	atmosphere	
1 ounce =	28.3495 grams	(atm)	

Relative density (SG)	Equivalent	1 technical atmosphere (at)	14.2233 lbf/in² (psi) 1 kgf/cm²
Pure water at 20°C	Specific gravity = 1.000 1 kilogram per litre 10.0224 pounds per imperial gallon 8.3454 pounds per US gallon		

To calculate the approximate underwater area of a yacht, and the quantity of paint required per coat, multiply the waterline length by the beam plus the draft. Multiply the figure by 0.5 for fin keeled racing yachts, by 0.75 for full bodied or bilge keeled yachts, or by 1.0 for motor cruisers. As an example:

Waterline length	9 m
Beam	2.5 m
Draft	1.5 m
Calculate 9 m × (2.5 m + 1.5 m) =	36
Multiplied by 0.6 (for a cruising yacht) =	21.6 m²
Divide this figure by the rate of paint coverage (ie 8 m²) =	2.7 litres per coat

To calculate the approximate topsides area (including transom), multiply the yacht's overall length by the maximum freeboard, and then double the figure. As an example:-

Overall length	12 m
Maximum freeboard	1.1 m
Calculate 12 m × 1.1 m × 2	26.4 m²
Divide this figure by the rate of paint coverage (ie 11 m²) =	2.4 litres per coat

Useful addresses

YACHT PAINT AND VARNISH MANUFACTURERS AND DISTRIBUTORS

United Kingdom

Blakes Paints
Swanwick Marina
Swanwick Shore Road
Southampton
Hampshire SO31 7EF
Tel: 01489 864440
Fax: 01489 564011
www.blakespaints.com

International Yacht Paints
24–30 Canute Road
Southampton
Hampshire SO9 3AS
Tel: 02380 226722
Fax: 02380 222090
www.yachtpaint.com

Jotun Paints
Stather Road
Flixborough
Lincolnshire DN15 8RR
Tel: 01724 400000
Fax: 01724 400100
www.jotun.co.uk
Jotun paints are available
throughout Europe, with limited
availability in the USA

Marineware
(Epifanes and Awlgrip
Distributors)
Unit 6, Crosshouse Centre
Crosshouse Road
Southampton, Hants SO14 5GZ
Tel: 02380 330208
Fax: 02380 339667
www.marineware.co.uk

SP Resin Systems Ltd (HQ)
St Cross Business Park
Newport
Isle of Wight PO30 5WU
Tel: 01983 828000
Fax: 01983 828100
www.spsystems.com
(Note: SP Systems products are
distributed in the UK by Blakes
Paints. They are also supplied
directly to the USA by
SP Systems.)

Wessex Resins and Adhesives Ltd
Cupernham House
Cupernham Lane
Romsey
Hants SO51 7LF
Tel: 01794 521111
Fax: 01794 517779
www.wessex-resins.com

USA

Epifanes North America Inc
c/o Mr Doug Theobald
58 Fore Street
Portland Main 04101 USA
Tel: +1 207 775 1333
Fax: +1 207 775 1551

Gougeon Brothers Inc
(West Systems)
PO Box 655
100 Patterson Avenue
Bay City
Michigan 48707 USA
Tel: +1 866 937 8797
Fax: +1 989 684 1374
www.westsystem.com

Interlux Yacht Finishes
2270 Morris Avenue
Union
New Jersey 07083 USA
Tel: +1 908 686 1300
Fax: +1 908 686 8545
www.yachtpaint.com

US Paints
(Awlgrip Yacht Finishes)
831 South 21st Street
St Louis
Missouri 63103
USA
Tel: +1 314 621 0525
Fax: +1 314 621 0722

VC Systems
See International Yacht Paints

CATHODIC PROTECTION ENGINEERS

United Kingdom

MG Duff Marine Ltd
Unit 2 West
68 Bognor Road
Chichester
West Sussex
PO19 2NS
Tel: 01243 533336
Fax: 01243 533422

MOISTURE METER MANUFACTURERS AND DISTRIBUTORS

United Kingdom

Sovereign Chemical
Industries Ltd
Park Road
Barrow in Furness
Cumbria
LA14 4QU
Tel: 01229 870880
Fax: 01229 870850
www.sovchem.co.uk

Tramex Ltd
Station House
Shankhill
Co Dublin
Eire
Tel: 00 353 1 282 3688
Fax: 00 353 1 282 7880
www.tramex.co.uk

UK Distributor for Tramex and
Sovereign Moisture Meters:
Nigel Clegg Associates
The Manor House
West End
Sedgefield
Co Durham
TS21 2BW
Tel: 01740 620489
Fax: 01740 620489
www.passionforpaint.co.uk

USA

Tramex USA
c/o Dennis Wieszcholek
Black Hawk Sales
28 Pin Oak Drive
Littleton
Colorado 80127 USA
Tel: +1 303 972 7926
Fax: +1 303 972 7106

SPRAY PAINTING AND SURFACE PREPARATION EQUIPMENT

United Kingdom

DeVilbiss Ransburg Industrial
Coating Equipment
Ringwood Road
Bournemouth
Dorset
BH11 9LH
Tel: 01202 571111
Fax: 01202 581940
www.devilbiss.co.uk

Hodge Clemco Ltd
Orgreave Drive
Sheffield
South Yorkshire
S13 9NR
Tel: 0114 2548811
Fax: 0114 2540250

Index